TIAGO BRUNET

PEOPLE
SPECIALIST

BIBLICAL SOLUTIONS FOR
REAL-LIFE RELATIONSHIPS

WHITAKER
HOUSE

All Scripture quotations are taken from the *Holy Bible, New International Version*®, NIV®, © 1973, 1978, 1984, 2011 by Biblica, Inc.® Used by permission. All rights reserved worldwide. The "NIV" and "New International Version" are trademarks registered in the United States Patent and Trademark Office by Biblica, Inc.®

Boldface type in the Scripture quotations indicates the author's emphasis.

Translation of *Especialista em pessoas* (Portuguese language edition of *People Specialist*) into English by Jorge Carmago.

PEOPLE SPECIALIST:
Biblical Solutions for Real-Life Relationships

ISBN: 979-8-88769-012-4
eBook ISBN: 979-8-88769-013-1
Printed in the United States of America
© 2023 by Tiago Brunet

Whitaker House
1030 Hunt Valley Circle
New Kensington, PA 15068
www.whitakerhouse.com

Library of Congress Control Number: 2022951536

1 2 3 4 5 6 7 8 9 10 11 ⨆ 30 29 28 27 26 25 24 23

CONTENTS

ACKNOWLEDGMENTS

To thank those who have contributed to my life, particularly with this project, would fill another book. Nobody accomplishes great things alone, and I am no exception. Many people have helped me. I'm the result of this joint effort.

I'm grateful to God for the privilege of having friends, partners, collaborators, team members, and family members who mold, propel, encourage, correct, and advise me.

I thank Jeanine, my wife, for the years she's believed in me and my ideas, even with all my limitations. Nine, you've always believed I could help people through my books. Thank you!

I thank my kids, who are the inspiration I need to go on. While I wrote this book, Jasmim, our fourth child, arrived. During the nine months of my wife's pregnancy, I remained focused on my computer and books, preparing this material for you!

Julia, José, Joaquim, and Jasmim: Daddy loves you!

I'm grateful to my editors Cassiano Elek Machado and Marilia Chaves (who believed in the theme of this book), Xavier Cornejo (who represents me abroad and advises me in international publications), and Gisele Romão (who reviewed this book and helped me with research). You encourage me, polish my material, and bring out the best in me. Thank you for your tips, dedication, corrections, and affection. Thanks to Editora Planeta for believing in this work and to Whitaker House for their commitment to making this book available to English-speaking readers.

I also thank my brother, Daniel Brunet, who always helped me to write with balance. And Marcos Simas, who believed in my potential and opened doors I never dreamed of entering.

If we were to remove from my life the people mentioned in these acknowledgments, this book would not be possible.

I need to honor the one who inspires me and gives me strength to be faithful to my purpose in life: the divine strength I know as the Holy Spirit.

As Jesus Himself said once, *"Apart from me you can do nothing"* (John 15:5).

I recognize this!

INTRODUCTION:
PEOPLE NEED PEOPLE

I receive thousands of messages through social media and am often stopped in public. Do you want to know what people say to me? They say things like this:

- ◆ "Tiago, please help me. I want to have success in life."
- ◆ "Tiago, I want to help change the world."
- ◆ "Tiago, I want to be relevant."

Everybody wants to be happy, and everybody wants to be successful. People imagine I can give them a secret recipe or formula, some quick advice offered in one of those passing airport conversations, that will allow them to achieve happiness and success. But the truth is that life is a process.

I've written numerous books, and in each one, I've given foolproof advice that helps people navigate through life, overcome obstacles, and emerge victorious. I help them to find their purpose, to develop emotional intelligence, to live out their own destiny (and not the destiny of others), to learn how to deal with money wisely, and to have the greatest power at their command.

I devoted the years of 2018 and 2019 to thinking about what gives meaning to life. I wanted to find a connection between the success stories, the extraordinary people who impacted mankind, the timeless lessons from the Bible, and the inevitable and rapid changes we see in the world. During this precious time of reflection devoted to broadening my knowledge, I found out we're all in search of answers and purpose. My questions about the reason for our existence and the euphoria we experience when we achieve success both had the same answer: *people*.

Nothing makes sense without them.

A DIFFICULT PARADOX

Joana, an angel God sent to help my wife Jeanine and me raise our four children, said something profound to me the other day: "It was a person who gave you the first bath in your life, and it will be a person who gives you your last one."

Her comment perfectly captured an insight I uncovered recently that has changed *everything*. Want to learn it? Here it is:

In the long run, people are the ones who will define whether our lives are worth living. People need people.

We need people!

It's sometimes difficult to accept this truth, especially in light of a second, equally truthful insight I've had:

People are difficult.

I once asked my followers on social media what they found to be the most difficult thing about dealing with people. I got all kinds of answers: lack of trust, disappointment, emotional wounds. What struck me was that 70 percent of the answers were the same and consisted of one word: *people*!

"My problem in dealing with people are the people!" stated one person.

People are complex. Each human being is shaped by different values, cultural influences, and stories. People's lived experiences define how they approach their time in the land of the living. As thinking and emotional beings, we connect to each other and make history together, but we don't have a clear idea of who other people really are. When we make ourselves emotionally vulnerable as we search for deep connections with others, we are at risk of getting hurt by those we trust the most. However, even when we are hurt, our humanity longs for connection. That's why we find it hard to let go of people who have wronged us. We remain connected to each other, both emotionally and spiritually, even when that connection causes us pain.

So there you have it—two seemingly conflicting truths: people need people in order to be happy, but dealing with people is difficult and causes us pain. Where do we go from here?

Life on earth is very short; we don't have time to spend our lives struggling with our relationships. We need help—some advice to simplify things for us. And that is the simple goal of this book: to give you suggestions for more easily navigating your relationships with other people.

WHO IS SHAPING YOUR STORY?

On September 15, 2008, the collapse of the real estate market in the United States launched a worldwide financial crisis. Stock exchanges around the world plummeted, capital disappeared, real estate investments devalued to absurd levels, and multinational companies crashed. One of the few industries that grew between 2003 and 2011—and it grew exponentially—was that of pet stores.[1]

What can we learn from this? *That people decided it's easier to deal with a pet than to try to understand other people.* There's a reason we think of dogs as man's best friend. For one, a dog is able to forgive quickly. You can scold a dog one minute, and the next minute, when you call him, he will happily come running back. Dogs keep no record of wrongs! For another, dogs are usually joyful and transform the environment where they live. Yes, we have much to learn from our pets.

Similarly, I've found that many people value material things more than their fellow man. Why? It's not because they are essentially materialistic—it's because they're less likely to get hurt by material possessions. They feel safer

---

1. Caitlin Moldvay, "IBISWorld Industry Report 45391: Pet Stores in the US," *Ibis World*, February 2012, http://big.assets.huffingtonpost.com/ibis.pdf.

caring for things because their things won't betray them. Things don't offend you, abandon you, or criticize you. Things don't react to what you say or do. You can use things anytime you want and set them aside whenever you choose without giving thought to their feelings.

Yet we must remember that, however difficult coexisting with other humans can be—and it can be difficult—*we will never change the world using things; we can only change the world by serving other people.* Things don't feel wronged by evil; it is people who are wronged and need others to fight for them. It is people—not things—who gather together to protest racism. The world needs good people more than it needs modern things.

You can love things, but they will never love you back. The decision to love and serve people—not things—is difficult but necessary.

Impossible as it might seem, getting along with other people is essential to our happiness. Sure, a pet can bring us joy; after all, it doesn't betray us, speak evil of us, or abandon us (most of the time). A new car can make our life easier. However, it is people who can make us happy and whole. Quite simply, *people need people!*

I'm sure that if you reflect on your best and worst memories, you'll see that both your best days and your worst days happened because of people. You weren't humiliated or abandoned by an animal or an object, but by people. You weren't cherished and encouraged by an animal or an object, but by people. Nobody wants to celebrate a great achievement alone in their car. The best wine does not come from Europe or a special harvest; rather, it is the wine that we have shared with an amazing person. We want to celebrate life's milestones surrounded by the people who are most important to us.

> ## Impossible as it might seem, getting along with other people is essential to our happiness.

In short, everything—*everything*—has to do with people.

I've had the opportunity to test this theory on individuals in different life situations (whether good or bad). I've talked to celebrities, highly successful businesspeople, people from different niches and varying levels of popularity—and absolutely everyone I've met has ended up, at some point in the conversation, saying something like, "So-and-so changed my life for the better," or "He (or she) was my downfall."

At some point, someone gets into your story—sometimes without being invited—and changes things. For the better or the worse, people define our future. Politicians may rule a country, but it is people who rule your inner world. Do you understand?

> ## Politicians may rule a country, but it is people who rule your inner world.

I don't know what your dream is, but you're certainly going to need people to make it come true! Many people dream of marriage; others prioritize their well-being; some chase financial gain; others just want to erase their past and have the opportunity to live better in the future. All of this, in the end, comes down to *people*. People are the ones who contribute to carrying out (or to hindering) our plans and projects. People are the ones who have hurt you; people are the ones who have been a source of healing in your life. Right?

> ## I don't know what your dream is, but you're certainly going to need people to make it come true!

Consider this: You've become a millionaire, and you're living on a spectacular island. On this island you have access to everything: the best houses, brand-new cars, and five-star restaurants. The only thing you won't have there is people. You'll have to enjoy all of this without a single person around.

So...are you in?

I think you get the idea. Now, the point is this: if your hopes for the future involve people, you'll need to learn to deal with people. This is what this book is all about!

BECOMING A PEOPLE SPECIALIST

When you invest in the stock exchange, you expect a return on your investment. When you invest in people, however, having high expectations may drag you down into a pit of disappointment. I invest in people daily—but I never expect anything in return.

> ## Invest in people, but don't expect anything from them.

Perhaps you're in a season where you're angry with someone. Perhaps you're not on speaking terms with a loved one. Perhaps your family dinners are rife with arguments and conflict. The people in our lives can be challenging, but, believe me, you need them.

Seeking to improve your relationships and mend those that are broken is a worthwhile investment of your time and energy. After all, the fewer enemies you have, the greater chance you'll have of finishing life well. Become a people specialist, and get ready to be a leader in whatever you do.

> ## Become a people specialist, and get ready to be a leader in whatever you do.

Unfortunately, this next generation has failed to grasp the secret to success. This generation has the power to "block" people on social media, and they have resorted to blocking people without moderation in real life, as well. It seems no one in this generation wants to actually *solve* their problems—silencing them is enough. But I can guarantee that this isn't an effective strategy. Those problems they've silenced are like ghosts: they will come back to haunt them. As Sigmund Freud said, "Unexpressed emotions will never die. They are buried alive and will come forth later in uglier ways."[2]

The doors of opportunity will open only once you understand that the people around you are the ones who will help or hinder your future. Once you accept this, the fear that paralyzes you and triggers your instinct of wanting to block your problems will disappear.

The president of Coca-Cola studied hard to become qualified for the position of CEO, but ultimately it was his relationship with a person that put him in the position he had always dreamed of. A solid CV is an asset, but good interpersonal relationships are the key to being helped by a top-class head-hunter. We can even find examples of networking success in the Bible: the famous Shadrach, Meshach, and Abednego were appointed chiefs of business in the thriving empire of Babylon because of their relationship to their friend Daniel. Things can make life easier, but only people can define our existence.

> ## Things can make life easier,
> ## but only people can define our existence.

Envious people will always exist; so will people characterized by resentment and paranoia. Pride, fear, insecurity, hatred—these will always be part of humanity. Unforgettable and unpleasant people have existed since throughout history. You will have to learn to deal with them. You will have to coexist with the worst parts of humanity.

Those who look upon you with envy will not stop doing so just because you don't like to be envied. The critic won't stop criticizing just because you're upset by their comments. You will have to be the one to change—to make it so that what comes from outside doesn't strike your inner spirit. As the title page suggests, this book is about people. It's about how we relate to people, how we understand people's motives. However, this book isn't solely focused on other people—in fact, it's mostly focused on ourselves. After all, the more we understand ourselves, the better we can understand others.

---

2. Quoted in Maryann Wei, "Not All Screams Are Heard," PsychCentral, January 3, 2017, https://psychcentral.com/blog/not-all-screams-are-heard#1.

People only change if you change. The solution is in you, not in someone else—believe me! So, how willing are you to foster changes in your life?

The solution is in you, not in someone else.

With the help of this book, you will:

+ Learn to survive envy, gossip, and intrigue (behaviors that will always exist);

+ Identify the unavoidable people in life and learn to deal with them;

+ Learn to let go of the wrong people in your life (this is really important);

+ Understand how to deal with the most difficult people (it's upsetting but necessary);

+ Learn to relate to others by order of priority;

+ Understand theories of people classification;

+ Understand and apply the three spheres of friendship (this will change you);

+ Have the wisdom to think and speak (after all, you're dealing with human beings);

+ Grasp the two-in-one theory: the difficult art of living as a couple (living alone usually is worse);

+ Learn to have principles that are stronger than your feelings;

+ Inoculate yourself against pride (this is surprising!);

+ Learn to move forward on the trail of life;

+ Observe with more wisdom the mirrors of life;

+ Be provided with ancient tools to solve current relationship problems.

How wonderful it is that you have this book in hand! I'm certain that if you keep your mind open and anticipate transformation as you read it, you won't be able to keep yourself from recommending it to those around you.

REAL VERSUS IDEAL

If my comments about how difficult people can be seem negative or pessimistic to you, you're not alone in your opinion. One time, after I posted on Instagram about how the theory of association explains why we have so many enemies (see chapter 1 for more on this), a woman in her fifties took offense. She declared unabashedly, "I don't have enemies. Jesus commanded us to love one another." As someone who has, by the grace of God, served as a spiritual guide to many, I found this woman's defense of her faith simply beautiful. However, it brings up a topic I'll emphasize throughout this book: the difference between the ideal world and the real world.

In the ideal world, people love each other; nobody judges anybody else. In the ideal world, we can rely on our family members to protect and support us, and we forgive without delay or resentment those who have offended or persecuted us.

However, in the real world, things don't quite work this way—at least not yet. In the real world, family members gossip, friends betray, and those who should love us abandon us instead. In the real world, envy is powerful, haters and critics operate at a professional level, and lies flow at the same speed as broadband Internet. In the real world, other people bring us more emotional distress than joy.

Can you relate?

It can feel a bit hopeless to conduct ourselves daily in this battle between "ideal" and "real." I believe this is the exact reason Jesus came to this earth: He saw that humans were in need of hope, and He came to point us to the future, ideal world.

Today, many of us live with our eyes gazing longingly at the promised ideal world, striving to exist as if we are already there. In reality, however, we need to protect our minds and hearts against real-world emotional epidemics that try to infect us. The world we're living in now is the real world. We need to learn how to survive in it.

This book has been written for this moment in time, for the life we are living today in the *real* world. However, please do not lose hope: the ideal world will one day become the real world, and at that time, all relationships will be perfect.

Until then, let this book serve as a guide for you to understand and relate to the people around you.

ABOUT THIS BOOK

For years I studied topics and obtained knowledge that I've rarely used. I memorized the square roots, I studied demonology, I learned the history of medieval Europe, and so on. But where was the class that would allow me to become an expert on those with whom I deal every single day—people? I've yet to find one.

Weird, isn't it?

With this book, I'm offering to you the guidance that I never received. I'm equipping you to improve your relationships with others. Because there is no denying that our relationships with others are difficult to navigate. Indeed, the closer a person is to us, the greater likelihood they have of hurting us. Why? *We share information about ourselves with those who are closest to us.* We share our pain, mistakes, secrets, and dreams with them. And this can become a kind of "trigger" against us later on! That's why, in chapter 1, we'll discuss three spheres of friendship that help us evaluate who should have access to the intimate details of our life.

Once we've established the three spheres of friendship in our lives, we'll spend several chapters distilling this simple piece of wisdom: the journey of life takes us on a road full of stones.

The journey of life takes us on a road full of stones.

The people in our lives are represented by stones: they are often uncomfortable and difficult to carry. They take various forms, serve varying purposes, and should be dealt with in unique ways. Some people are stumbling blocks; others are pebbles in our shoes; others are essential blocks in helping us build success. The one thing that is true of all stones is that they are simply inevitable. Stones on the road will always exist. The Brazilian poet Carlos Drummond de Andrade captures this idea well in his poem "No meio do caminho." The first stanza of this poem translates as follows:

> In the middle of the road there was a stone.
> there was a stone in the middle of the road
> there was a stone
> in the middle of the road there was a stone.
>
> Never should I forget this milestone....[3]

Yes, stones are an inevitable part of life. Sometimes they insist on being part of our journey. These stones are generally people who are close to us, such as our relatives; some of these people constitute the "unavoidable ones" we will discuss in chapter 2. Others are easily removed from our lives, like a pebble we can pluck from our shoe. In chapter 3, we'll discuss in greater detail how to go about removing the "avoidable ones" from our lives. Some are gems we put in our pocket and incorporate permanently into our life's journey. The intricacies and challenges of living the two-in-one life this choice demands are the focus of chapter 4. Still other stones are rocks embedded in our path that cause us to trip and stumble. We'll discuss how to deal with such thieves of joy—and to protect ourselves while doing so—in chapter 5.

Other stones are helpful to us, as they can serve as building blocks to success. We should utilize and maintain our relationships with such stones. They are opportunities disguised as people. Indeed, you only "get there" with the help of people.

We shouldn't give up on people, though at times we'll be tempted to do so. In the remaining chapters, we'll examine in greater depth one of the greatest obstacles we face in our relationships with others: ourselves. In chapter 6, we'll learn to identify the different stages of our journey through life and consider how our current stage can impact our relationships with those closest to us. In chapter 7, we'll explore how improving ourselves can equip us to better relate

---

3. Carlos Drummond de Andrade, "In the Middle of the Road," translation by Heloisa Prieto; available at Harry Browne, "In the Middle of the Road by Carlos Drummond de Andrade," *Inksplinters*, October 31, 2018, https://inksplinters.wordpress.com/2018/10/31/in-the-middle-of-the-road-by-carlos-drummond-de-andrade/.

to others. Finally, in chapter 8, I'll present to you three basic pillars that are essential when you find yourself in times of conflict or struggle.

When I tested the theories I present in this book on my social media networks, many people questioned my ideas. That's to be expected: the paradigms I present are probably different from anything you've encountered before. Sometimes, my ideas stand in opposition to culturally accepted norms. It's important to remember that our understanding of the world, like beauty, is in the eye of the beholder.

> ## Transform your mind.
> ## Let it open to new ideas and possibilities.

If you cling to the vision you have today, you will, at most, be able to maintain the life you already have. But if you want to move forward and grow, be prepared to change your way of thinking. Transform your mind. Let it open to new ideas and possibilities.

THE PATH FORWARD

When I was a teen, I would often pray, "Lord, give me wisdom." I believe God heard my prayer. I've grown so much in wisdom and experience since then. Everything I share in this book is based on my studies and research. I was ordained to the pastoral ministry thirteen years ago, and during the years since then I have served and worked alongside a wide array of people. Prior to that, I was a businessman. Over the past four years, I've worked as a life and business coach, serving celebrities, professional soccer players, and highly successful businesspeople. I've learned so much from my experience both as a pastor and coach, and I'm eager to share my insights with you.

In this book, I will present to you biblical solutions for real world social-emotional problems. I am a theologian by background and a researcher of Scripture by passion. Thus, the solutions I present in this book will always be biblical. I think biblical solutions are the only ones worth pursuing. After all, the teachings we find in Scripture have been working for centuries—why try to reinvent the wheel? Why follow some untried theory when the scriptural one is proven to be effective? The best investment is the one guaranteed to be profitable! I suggest you have a Bible next to you while you read this book. I include many biblical references so that you can study what we discuss here in greater depth.

Your real world will be much better after you learn how to coexist with those who are closest to you. After all, you're not going to go far in life if you don't have people at your side. If you're reading this book coming from a place of hurt, you may find it difficult to agree with this truth. Let's take a deep breath and move forward together, blazing the trail of this social-emotional universe in which human relationships exist.

Some people hurt; others heal.

After reading this book, decide whether you will be the one who hurts or the one who heals. The one who disturbs or the one who makes things easier. Choose the best path! Let's set forth together in search of the ideal world.

I wish you peace and prosperity.
Tiago Brunet

1

THE THREE SPHERES OF FRIENDSHIP

"Friendship is what makes our difficult moments bearable
and our good moments memorable."
—Author Unknown

Celebrate those who come into your life; don't complain about those who left."

I said this in one of my most popular videos on the Internet. It was the first video I had go viral. The thoughts I put forth in it resonated so strongly with people that this one post had around thirty-million views. This certainly caught my attention!

I've noticed that the videos I post about *people* receive about 300 percent higher engagement than my other content. Why? That's easy. Who has never been disappointed by a friend? Who has never had a conflict with a coworker? Who has never struggled to relate to their parents?

The answer is no one.

Friendships can bring us indescribable joy—or tremendous sorrow. People are unpredictable; you never know when a so-called friend will stab you in the back. Because of this, many of us have heaps of memories with friends marked by anger and resentment; our friendships are rife with disagreements.

The fact is that people won't change simply because you don't like them. *It takes specific knowledge, patience, and wisdom to bring about changes in someone.* Usually, the change has to start from within yourself.

Are you ready to make the changes necessary to improve your friendships?

FAIR-WEATHER FRIENDS

In 2014, when my company went bankrupt, I entered a period of deep distress. Not only was I facing exorbitant debt, but when I looked around, I found I had almost no friends left. During that time, I was able to truly understand the Bible verse that says, *"A friend loves at all times, and a brother is born for a time of adversity"* (Proverbs 17:17).

Those who decided to leave me back then have receded into my distant memory. On the other hand, the friend who stayed…? This man became part of my family—*"a brother"*—and now holds a special place in my heart. Those who stand beside us on our most difficult days, when we're in anguish, deserve a starring role in the movie of our lives.

Even Jesus Christ, who never let anyone down and who trained His twelve dearest friends for three years, was ruthlessly betrayed by one of His closest companions. (See Matthew 26:14–16, 47–50.) Another friend—one of His closest friends, in fact—openly denied three times that he knew Him, just because he was afraid of getting in trouble by association. (See Luke 22:54–62.) When Jesus went through His most difficult and painful experience—death on a cross—only one of His many friends and followers stayed to offer Him support. (See John 19:25–27.)

If a single man who had had never committed any act of evil in His life experienced so much hurt and abandonment from His friends, imagine how much more we mere mortals, in all our brokenness, will experience!

On good days, it's almost impossible to identify someone's true intentions. Human beings are so dramatic and complex, and everything can be staged. On bad days, however, there isn't a single person capable of pretending. In our worst times, we recognize people for who they truly are.

Outsiders and acquaintances might just disappoint us, but those who eat at our table and are privy to our secrets can betray us deeply. Whatever the level of intimacy, any relationship can cause us pain. In this first chapter, we will explore the three spheres of friendship and learn how correctly categorizing our friends can prevent us from undergoing unnecessary anguish.

INTIMATE, NECESSARY, STRATEGIC

My belief that our relationships with people are key to a life lived well has evolved from my familiarity with the ancient and sacred Word of God. In fact, the theory I'm about to present—the theory of the three spheres of friendship—is inspired by Christ's journey here on earth; that's why I'm sure it's an unfailing theory.

Every day I learn new things from the life of the Man from Nazareth. When I studied Jesus's life to see what it could teach us about friendship, I noticed that the people He interacted with fell into three main spheres. Let's take a look.

1. **Strategic:** Jesus had five hundred followers who were His *strategic* friends. When Jesus went up to heaven, these five hundred served as eyewitnesses who would spread the news of His life, death, and resurrection over all the earth. (See 1 Corinthians 15:6.) We all need strategic friends. These friends might not eat at your table or watch the same shows as you on Netflix, but they are important connections who will be essential in building up your future.

2. **Necessary:** Jesus had twelve *necessary* friends. Without them, He wouldn't have had a team. (See Luke 6:12–16.) Like Jesus did, you also need friends. Not all of them will your best friends or your closest friends, but they are still necessary to your walk down the road of life.

3. **Intimate:** Jesus had three close, *intimate* friends. These were the people with whom Jesus would entrust His secrets and share His dreams. He revealed who He really was to these three friends, His inner circle. For instance, when He went to the Mount of Transfiguration, Jesus invited only His inner circle to accompany Him and witness the event. (See Matthew 17:1–13.)

Here is one of the secrets to happiness: learning to "classify" your friends. Which sphere does each of your friends fall into? Intimate? Necessary? Or strategic? When you sort each friend into their proper sphere, you set an appropriate level of expectation for that relationship. You can then recognize how much their flaws will affect you. In the long term, this will help you to suffer less because lower expectation equals less disappointment.

Let's see how this worked in the life of Jesus by examining His friendships with two people: Judas and Peter.

Judas betrayed Jesus. As a member of the Twelve, he was in the sphere of Jesus's necessary friends.

Peter denied Jesus. As one of Jesus's three closest friends, he was in the sphere of intimate friends.

The level of expectation for a necessary friend is different from that of an intimate friend.

Lower expectation = less disappointment.

When Judas went to the garden of Gethsemane to hand over the Master with a kiss, Jesus was not surprised. He merely replied, *"Do what you came for, friend"* (Matthew 26:50). It's sad, but the Nazarene had already expected to be betrayed. Perhaps that's why He had never shared His intimate secrets with Judas and is not recorded moping over this betrayal later on.

If a betrayal of this degree ever happened to me, I think I would be saying for years, "It's all Judas fault!" "Ah, if only Judas hadn't done that!" or "Out! Out! Away with you, Judas!" Why do we get so frustrated with our friends, despite their flaws, if Jesus was not frustrated by His friend's terrible betrayal?

Here's the difference: Jesus had adjusted His expectations of Judas because He knew which sphere of friendship Judas belonged in. This knowledge shielded Him from feeling deeply hurt when His necessary friend turned against Him.

Do you have an emotional shield up that will protect you from moping for years over wrongdoings and mistakes others have made that have impacted you?

Our friends, no matter how close they are, are still humans and are thus prone to fail. But a close friendship carries distinct traces. We see this in Jesus's friendship with His intimate friend Peter. Scripture records that Peter denied Jesus not once but *three times* in a single night! His actions after that point, however, are what distinguish him from those in the other two spheres of friendship. He repented immediately, cried bitterly, and sought reconciliation. (See Matthew 26:69–75.)

LET OFFENSE BE SWEPT AWAY

Let me tell you a popular story about friendship.

Two friends are traveling in a desert. In the middle of this difficult journey through inhospitable terrain, they argue and start to fight. The first friend slaps the other across the face. The friend who has been slapped says nothing. He doesn't strike back. He only bends down and writes in the sand: "Today, my best friend slapped me across the face."

Things are tense, but they have a journey to complete, so they move on. After a while, they reach an oasis. Ah, how refreshing after such a long, difficult trip! They both dive into the water for a celebratory swim.

Suddenly, the friend who had been slapped across the face starts to drown. The friend who struck him, the aggressor, risks his own life to save him.

After he recovers from the shock of the incident, the friend who had been slapped digs his penknife from his pocket and carves into a rock: "Today, my best friend saved my life."

Intrigued, the one who risked his life to save his friend asks, "After I attacked you, you wrote in the sand, and now that I have saved you, you wrote on the rock. Why?"

The other replies, "When a close friend offends us, we should write of the offense on the sand, for there the wind of forgetfulness and forgiveness ensures that the offense will be erased. However, when a friend does something great for us, we should write of it on a rock and carve it into our memories and into our hearts, for there, neither wind nor time will be able to erase the marks of the good received."

The bottom line is this: even our closest friends may wrong us. Bear in mind that no human being is perfect. What really matters is how you choose to record this error. Commit to memory only the good things of life. Don't cling to the negative. Allow all evil to be swept away by the wind and by forgiveness.

It is only when we cross the deserts in life that we know the best of us and the worst of us.

ATTRACTION AND SELECTION

Is there some kind of power that attracts people to you and allows you to make friends? Of course, there is! People are drawn to what attracts them. Consider the animal world. It's because of attraction that a fisherman is able to catch a fish. Fish will never get close to a fisherman's hook if he doesn't place bait on it to draw their interest.

The average fisherman knows he needs to use bait to attract fish. The great fisherman knows *what kind* of bait to use to catch the *right kind of fish*.

When we think about making friends, it's not about quantity. We need to think about quality. Because just like there are fish that we'd rather toss back into the ocean than eat, there are friends who we'd rather keep at an arm's length than develop intimacy with.

We've all had encounters with "bad fish." Perhaps it is someone who gets close to us only because they want something from us. These types of people are egoistic, and fostering friendships with them tends to be a mistake! Or perhaps it is someone who is in desperate need of fast companionship but has no interest in truly knowing and caring for you. These types will abandon you on a whim.

The logical question, then, is to ask: What do you need to have to attract the right people to your life? What does it take to fill your network of friends? It can include:

+ Attraction

+ Maintenance

+ Money

+ Behavior

+ Status quo

+ Character

+ Networking

+ Reciprocity

+ Social media

+ Level of attention

+ Charisma

+ Truth

+ Titles

+ Feedback

+ Abilities

+ Social encounters

Let me offer two examples from my own life of how friendships are made. When I moved away from Brazil, I had to start over in some parts of my life. Some of my friendships with people from Brazil and other parts of the world remained steady and solid, but I knew I would have to make new connections in the United States. After all, no one survives alone in this real and cruel world. Determined to build my network of friends, I set about casting lines.

The first friendship I forged had, as its base, *reciprocity*, *abilities*, and *social media*. As soon as our moving truck arrived and we began to unpack and settle into our new house, our American neighbors came over to offer cookies and a welcoming smile. In *reciprocation*, I gave them one of my books, which allowed them to easily search the Internet to find out who I am and what I do.

It turns out, my work accomplishments (*abilities*) and social media profiles (*social media*) served as great bait! That same week, some neighborhood kids were already playing with my children at the swimming pool. Thanks to their small gesture and my response to it, I soon had someone to chat with as I headed out the door for my morning appointments, and my kids had friends to play with on our street.

Another friend came into my life through a business meeting. A friendship based on *networking*, *abilities*, and *social media* evolved into one based on *mutual attraction* and *shared interests*. This friend initially reached out to me because, based on my professional achievements and social media presence, he saw a business opportunity. I, in turn, agreed to meet with him because he was a renowned businessman.

As he researched me further in preparation for our meeting, he ended up watching a video that transformed his way of thinking and broke a powerful paradigm in his life. As a result, he became a fan! Consequently, in our first meeting, he spent more time asking me questions than talking business. He saw me as a potential mentor. His desire to learn from me caught my attention. Over time, our business meetings turned into personal conversations at a local coffee shop. Eventually, true friendship set in.

There you have it. He drew closer to me because he wanted mentorship, and I drew closer to him because he was a well-known businessman. We shared common interests. The result? Coexistence by affinity and the birth of a new friendship!

Let's think about what happens if, instead of using a baited hook and line, the fisherman uses a net. When he casts his net, the fisherman is not sure what he will catch. As he lifts it out of the water, he may find all kinds of fish— and sometimes other kinds of aquatic animals. It is at this point that sorting becomes necessary. The fisherman must separate what serves from what he will give back to the sea.

I don't know how it is where you live, but we Brazilians are net-casters. We have the ability to become close friends with someone we've just met. It's not unusual to be introduced to a person one morning, and to have that same person in your home enjoying some barbecue that same afternoon. There's beauty in this ability, but it is not without its dangers. This social-emotional state can generate an excess of intimacy with people with whom you would *never* share your failures, secrets, and flaws.

Not everyone who "falls in your net" should stay there. Having too many friends often means having poor-quality friendships. I should note that I'm not encouraging you to become a closed-off person who blocks out others and makes friendship impossible. My purpose here is to teach how to be *selective*.

Learning how to categorize your friendships may save your life!

STRATEGIC FRIENDS

It was a pleasantly rainy Monday afternoon in the city of São Paulo—a perfect day for a coffee and a good book. I was euphoric as the date of a huge event, Transformation Day in Boston, drew closer. Transformation Day had already occurred in other cities, both Brazilian and American, but this would be the first time I would take part in this event of personal transformation in the northern United States.

Suddenly, my phone rang. "Tiago, Tiago!" the voice on the other end said. "It went all wrong with the venue. They can't rent the auditorium to you anymore."

"What? What place are you talking about, man?"

"The one for the event in Boston. We'll have to cancel it."

"Oh, no. It can't be!" I placed my hands in my head, as we all do without meaning to whenever we get bad news, and sighed.

Later that day, I explained to a close friend what was going on. When I finished, he said, "Well, I know someone in Boston who has an auditorium. Perhaps it will work. Shall we try talking to him?"

"Of course, yes!" I replied, my excitement returning.

On that day, I was introduced to a person who would take part in great moments of my life. We've laughed together more times than we can count. However, at that moment, as we were introduced by a video call and soon finalized a rental agreement, I had no idea that, months later, he would enter into my circle of very close friends. All I knew was that, as we exchanged our first words, I started to like him right away.

On the week of the event, I flew from São Paulo to the beautiful city of Boston. On a cold day (41 degrees Fahrenheit—the perfect temperature to me), this new friend introduced me to the city and brought me and my team to the venue so that we could finalize plans for the big event.

Here's the thing: this friend had decided to open the doors of his auditorium to me not because I was nice and friendly. No, he saw in me a possibility for growth. He knew what the event meant. He had already seen our work through social media and was sure hosting us would be to his advantage.

Likewise, I would not have met or drawn closer to this guy if he didn't have access to the venue I needed so badly for that day. He was the solution to a huge problem.

We worked together during that week toward or own goals. We were not enemies, nor were we strangers. We were friends, albeit newly introduced. However, the reason for our friendship was strategic.

I have many strategic friends in my life. Some have crossed the border and become necessary in my journey. Others have had access to my heart and today are counted among my close friends. But they all started out as strategic.

FRIENDS FOR A SEASON

What is a strategic friend?

Strategic friends don't love you (at least not yet). They don't cheer or get excited only by what you represent. Rather, they partner with you for a greater good—for something that may benefit you both. Strategic friends get closer on behalf of a common conquest.

Let's look at this another way. When you're building a house, you need scaffolding to accomplish several tasks, such as painting the walls and the ceiling, raising an upper deck, and installing lamps. The scaffolding is essential to your work. Without it, your tasks are harder and more dangerous.

However, when the building work is finished and the decorative phase begins, the scaffolding loses its purpose. It has not betrayed or beaten you. It's been faithful, but, in this next phase, it is of no use. It doesn't have any function.

Do you understand?

I should stress that I'm not comparing people to objects; rather, I'm illustrating their similar function. Scaffolding is useful in construction work but not for decoration. Likewise, there are people God allows to stay for a certain period in our lives for a strategic reason. They help us, they contribute—but only for a time. Don't insist on trying to retain them when God Himself decides to take them away.

We find examples of scaffolding or strategic friends in the Bible. Lot, Abraham's nephew, was a strategic friend to Abraham (see Genesis 13–14), while Laban, Jacob's father-in-law, was a strategic friend to Jacob (see Genesis 27–31). These men served important functions in these patriarchs' lives for a season, but once that season had passed, they were no longer part of their journey.

Some people fulfill a function in our destiny during our time on the earth. When their purpose in relation to our lives is complete, we need to learn to say good-bye.

SELF-INTEREST OR STRATEGY?

Many times we get hurt because we don't know the theory of the three spheres of friendship. We suffer by telling secrets or revealing dreams to someone who is not an intimate friend but only a strategic friend. These people are not our friends simply because they admire our dreams or our character; they are our friends because we can help each other reach our goals.

"But, Tiago, aren't these people simply motivated by self-interest?" you may ask. Possibly. But you need to understand that not all self-interested people are our enemies. In every relationship, without exception, there are personal interests involved.

Every relationship, consciously or unconsciously, starts with a strategy. Think about it: You may have married for love, but when you first met your spouse, you wanted to get to know that person better because of their physical attractiveness, or their laugh, or their confidence. Even our choice to seek God could have started with some self-interest. Perhaps you started going to church and searching for God because you had an interest in eternal salvation or you needed to solve some seemingly impossible problem.

This is just the way things are in the world we live in today. In the ideal world, this wouldn't happen—but, remember, we live in the real world. Recognizing that self-interest is at the base of many relationships doesn't turn you into a bad person; it reveals your humanity.

NECESSARY FRIENDS

When I was researching in preparation for writing this book, I interviewed a Brazilian billionaire whose family was ranked by *Forbes* magazine; a few years ago, he was considered the best CEO in the country. During the nearly four hours we spent together, I learned many things, but one phrase he said really caught my attention: "It is better to become friends with the people with whom you work than to try to work with people who are already your friends."

Wow! That made so much sense to me and helped me understand the sphere of necessary friends. Not everybody will be our close friends, but without necessary friends, what fun would life be?

We need people to make us happy. We need people to share our daily existence. We need friends at work. We need faithful clients. We need people who make us laugh. Necessary friends don't love you for who you are, but they stand by your side because of who or what you represent.

Consider Jesus's twelve necessary friends. We know them as the twelve apostles. Those men were concerned with things like the fulfillment of promises and who would sit next to Jesus on His heavenly throne. (See, for example, Mark 10:35–45.) At first, their hearts didn't belong to Jesus Himself but to the things He represented—and He represented an eternal kingdom. Nonetheless, they were His friends, and the Master needed them. Each one had an important role in Christendom.

NOT CLOSE, BUT STILL VITAL

Necessary friends are such an important category of friends. They are vital to our journey on this earth. Necessary friends are those who attend our birthday parties and weekend barbecues; they are the people we chat with during a fundraiser for a nonprofit we support or our organization's Christmas dinner; they are our neighbors and coworkers and fellow volunteers. These people keep our social lives active.

I have several childhood friends, most of whom are not intimate. I don't call them when I'm distressed or about to sign a big contract. However, they are essential in my life and necessary to my well-being. It's great to get together with them and reminisce about our childhoods. We spend hours laughing at the stupid things we used to do.

Yes, this category of friends is so important. Yet sometimes our hearts are deceitful and make us believe that if someone is not a close friend and 100 percent trustworthy, then they are not our friend. In the real world, it's not this way. We have to keep people around, even if we can't tell them everything about our lives.

We tend to mix things up, and that's where things go wrong. We want to do business with our close friends because we trust them. And we want to tell secrets to our necessary friends. With this kind of confusion between spheres, we cause ourselves distress. We often lack the maturity to separate people into their proper categories.

Keep on laughing with your necessary friends, but don't tell then your dreams; give them a hug, but don't reveal your heart to them; share the table with them, but don't confide in them what your next steps will be. Above all, cherish your necessary friends, because they are essential in your life.

ANDREW

Do you know who Andrew was?

Andrew, a former disciple of John the Baptist, was one of the first followers of Jesus. As soon as he met the Man of Nazareth, his eyes were fixed on Him in such a way that he could never leave Him.

Andrew was a great point of connection between people and Jesus's ministry. In fact, Andrew was the one who introduced his brother Peter to Christ—the same Peter who would become the patriarch of the Christian church. (See John 1:40–42.)

Nevertheless, although he was really a friend of the Master, Andrew was not part of Jesus's circle of close friends. Imagine if Andrew went about complaining, "I met Jesus first, I introduced people to Him, and now I'm not even closest to Him? He picked Peter over me as His close friend? I feel so used. These guys are all the same." Scripture doesn't record Andrew expressing any discontentment over his relationship with Jesus. He recognized that Jesus had both close friends and intimate friends, and he accepted his status with maturity.

Friendships that work take *maturity*. Without emotional balance and wisdom, we will never cultivate true friendships in any of the three spheres.

I have friends with whom I spend time, but I don't share with them all the details of my life or my dreams and secrets. It takes wisdom to respect the spheres. It takes maturity not to speak too much or expect something from someone who can't give it.

WITHOUT DEFENSE

Schindler's List is a great movie about a German businessman who saved the lives of many Jews during World War II. One scene depicts several Jewish prisoners being interrogated. A theft has been committed, and the Nazi officers are determined to find the thief.

When nobody confesses to guilt, the Nazi captain pulls one of the men out of the line and kills him. He makes it clear that until the thief surrenders himself or is identified by his companions, this tragedy will be repeated.

The captain points his gun at another man in the group and asks again who the thief is. A little boy takes a hesitant step forward. "Was it you?" demands the officer.

Trembling, with his head down, the boy just points to the dead man. By incriminating the one who has already died, the boy saves the rest of them.

What can we learn from this story? Guilt is usually thrown on one who can't defend himself. People are like this—it's just a fact we need to learn.

NECESSARY NEIGHBORS AND THE EVIL DAY

My neighbor is my friend. He is absolutely necessary in my life. We love each other and have lots of fun together. From time to time, we get our families together to cook a meal. Our wives chat in the living room while we grill. We also help each other out: he takes care of my garden when I travel, and I repay him in whatever way I can (sometimes with VIP tickets to see the Orlando Magic). This give-and-take is part of living in the real world. In the ideal world, people would help each other without expecting anything in return. In the real world, however, we get disappointed if we take a gift to our neighbor's birthday party but he doesn't bring one to ours. Am I right?

You might be thinking, "Tiago, this guy comes to your house and is close with your family, yet you're saying he isn't a close friend? What distinguishes a necessary friend from a close friend?"

The distinguishing factor is what I call the "evil day." A necessary friend's behavior in this season of your life determines whether they remain a necessary friend or get promoted to the next sphere.

An evil day is the day you get the worst news of your life. It's when you see a doctor and receive the worst diagnosis, or when you realize your company has collapsed. It's when you suddenly lose everything you've fought your whole life to build.

On that day—the day of trouble, of despair—save a little of your strength to notice who remains by your side.

Another way a necessary friend can become a close friend is by earning our trust. I sometimes determine whether a necessary friend is "close friend material" through subtle tests. For example, I'll share a story or a secret with a necessary friend—something private but not very sensitive (so I won't be affected if it leaks), something I haven't told anybody else. If what we talked about in private becomes public, I will know that he should remain among my necessary friends. If he keeps the information private, I'll know I can take a step further in our intimacy. I've done this test a couple of times and can assure you that it works!

Remember, friendship spheres are not set in stone. It's possible to move to another sphere, whether forward or backward. Keep in mind the advice I've already mentioned: *"A friend loves at all times, and a brother is born for a time of adversity"* (Proverbs 17:17).

CLOSE FRIENDS

You can usually count the number of your close friends on one hand. Not everyone has enough love and wisdom to be someone else's close friend—and love and wisdom are essential characteristics of candidates for close friendship. A member of someone's inner circle needs a great deal of love to gently alert their friend when they've made a mistake, and they need wisdom to keep their friends' secrets and advise them in hard times.

Having an inner circle is not a privilege but a matter of survival. We all need someone to call on, to confide in, to reveal secrets to, to dream with; we all need someone whose shoulder we can cry on. This is a *need*. And if this need isn't met, there can be serious emotional and social consequences.

Close friends don't make an impression by their achievements but by their character. They like to listen rather than speak. They don't care about being "pampered" by you, for they value your presence over your presents.

JOHN

Now, take my word—and forgive me if I'm being repetitive—that *"a brother is born for a time of adversity"* (Proverbs 17:17). A close friend is the one who stayed by your side during your hardest battle and remained there when the battle was lost.

Can you think of such a friend in your life?

Do you know who John was?

John, the youngest of Jesus's disciples, was also the closest to Jesus. He was the only one among the Twelve who stayed with the Master until the end of His mission. At the foot of the cross were huddled Mary, some other women, and John. (See John 19:25–26.)

Who was the most loving among the apostles and disciples of Christ? John. Who heard the largest number of secrets from Jesus? John. In fact, the mysteries of Revelation, the end of times, were entrusted to him. John was close enough to Jesus to feel comfortable laying his head on Jesus's chest and asking Him about the man who would betray the Master: *"Lord, who is it?"* (John 13:25). As Jesus faced His most difficult battle, guess who was the only among His friends who was still there? John.

John was truly *"a brother…born for a time of adversity"* (Proverbs 17:17). May we all find such a friend!

WORTHY OF TEARS

What should we say about Lazarus? Jesus cared deeply for His friend Lazarus and wept when He learned of His friend's death, temporary though it was. (See John 11:1–46.)

Some people enter into your life and win your heart. It is these people—rather than the ones who hurt you—whom you should cry for. Give away your thoughts and your time to those who treat you well, not to those who steal your peace and your joy.

SETTING REALISTIC EXPECTATIONS

"But, Tiago, won't even my close friends wrong me at some point?"

Yes, there is a 100 percent chance that they will. Create realistic expectations so that you won't be disappointed to the point of devastation. Friends are not perfect. They are human beings, and human beings tend to make mistakes. For this reason, we shouldn't put our full trust in any person—even a close friend—no matter how tempted we are to do so. If history shows us anything, it is that God will always be the *only* one we can truly trust. (See Psalm 41:9.)

Consider the following Bible verse:

*Cursed is the one who trusts in man, who draws strength from mere flesh
and whose heart turns away from the LORD.*   (Jeremiah 17:5)

This verse from Jeremiah states the folly of trusting in people, but it goes a
step further, describing the painful reality of one *"whose heart turns away from
the LORD."* When it comes to relationships with people in this life, a principle
I've learned is this: *peace comes from God.* So if you're not doing well with God,
you won't do well with anyone because you will never have peace.

Let's summarize what I'm saying:

+ If you're always fighting with God, how will you be at peace with other
  people?

+ If you don't understand God's forgiveness and love toward you, how
  will you love and forgive people?

*Bear with each other and forgive one another if any of you has a grievance
against someone. Forgive as the Lord forgave you.*   (Colossians 3:13)

THE END OF A FRIENDSHIP

How do we go about ending a friendship, and what would justify our
doing so?

Ending friendships can be painful. I once decided to stop talking to three
very close friends who had been, at least theoretically, part of my inner circle.
During that time, I came to understand that knowing the heart of those who
claim to be close friends is essential for a healthy life.

I truly believe God speaks with human beings. I personally have heard
His incomparably sweet voice. He also speaks through signals, dreams, feelings in our hearts, other people's words, and many other ways. One day, I
experienced a strong feeling in my heart. The idea came to me, strong and certain, that I must stop talking to those three close friends. I didn't cut them off
through any grand confrontation; I just subtly shifted how I related to them.
Over the course of four months, I greeted them normally and kept punctually
replying to their WhatsApp messages—but I wasn't as exuberant as I had
been before.

Silence reveals who people are.

Each friend had the same level of friendship with me and shared similar intimacy and closeness with me. Each one, however, reacted differently to my "forced silence."

The first one—let's call him Friend A—simply didn't react. He didn't approach me or ask me what was going on. However, he would ask our other friends, "Is Tiago okay? Is he talking to you like normal?"

Silence reveals who people are.

The second one, Friend B, distanced himself from me and started gossiping and speaking ill about me. "You see, Tiago is proud. He must be in trouble." "Tiago is a false friend. He abandons people from his past." "Tiago is lost. He doesn't know what he wants." This friend also attacked me publicly.

Unlike the first two, the third one, Friend C, tried to bridge the gap I'd created. The more I would recede into silence, the more frequently he would call me, ask if our families could get together, and suggest we meet when we found ourselves at the same airport (we both traveled a lot).

When those four months were over, I called each friend to talk. I rebuked Friend A, the one who hadn't reacted, saying, "You could have called me instead of asking others about me! We're friends, after all!" This wake-up call allowed us to continue our friendship.

I wished Friend B, the one who attacked me, the best of luck in everything, but I ended our friendship. After all, I can and must choose who sits at my table. I did so in a way that allowed us to remain civil; there is no resentment or rudeness between us. When we run into each other, I greet him and smile. I don't speak evil of him, not even when someone tries to provoke me to do so. I have simply recategorized him from close friend to a former friend.

The third one, Friend C, is no longer just my friend—today he is like a brother to me.

Everything in this life depends on people. Only when you learn to deal with them wisely will you find happiness.

THE THEORY OF ASSOCIATIONS

There is an ancient Sanskrit proverb that says, "The enemy of my enemy is my friend." Some people take issue with this proverb. However, if you think about all that we've discussed in this chapter, you will probably agree with me that in the real world, this proverb holds true.

I remember that during the Brazilian elections in 2018, which were marked by intense emotions and hatred, I posted a photo of the Brazilian flag on my Instagram with the caption, "Brazil, look upwards! There is a chance of being happy again." The quote came from the song "Brazil, Look Upwards" by João Alexandre.

Guess what happened?

Haters associated the Brazilian flag in my post with a controversial candidate who used the flag's colors in his motto, and they launched a series of social-media attacks against me. I've never experienced so much hatred first-hand. The only thing I did was post an image of my country's flag.

That's the way the theory of association works. When you post a photo of yourself with someone on social media, you're seen as taking a side and making a stand (even unconsciously). You're associating yourself with this person. In turn, this person's friends may start to like you—and their enemies may start to hate you, although you aren't "guilty" of anything." Right or wrong, this is just the reality of life. Relationships and emotion-driven people work this way, exactly as that ancient proverb says.

In the ideal world, of course, this wouldn't happen. In the ideal world, we would love each other according to Jesus's instructions; we would never judge others, nor would others judge us. However, as I've been emphasizing, the real world is different from the ideal world. We live in anticipation of a better world, but until that world becomes a reality, we have to live in the one we have.

Many people stopped following me because, in their view, I was taking a specific political side (even though I wasn't). Others cheered me on and shared my post.

There was no use in engaging in self-pity. There was no use in even trying to apologize; protesting with phrases such as "But I didn't know!" or "I have nothing to do with that!" wouldn't sway my newly made enemies. Don't be naïve. The world of today rejects those who claim ignorance.

> Don't be naïve. The world of today rejects those who claim ignorance.

I had to learn the hard way to be more intentional regarding my associations: the photos I take, the posts I publish, the lunches and parties I go to.

Everything is an association.

PRACTICING EMPATHY

A friend in my inner circle is a public figure—and a controversial one. No matter how diligently we avoid being photographed together, many people know we're friends and brothers. The issue of association with this friend becomes evident when an event I'm supposed to speak at is suddenly canceled after the organizer finds out I'm close friends with such a controversial figure. (To be clear, I'm not always the victim of the theory of association. I also find myself moving away from people who were probably fine but who lived in conflict with a friend of mine.)

I sometimes choose to take risks when it comes to my friendships, no matter the sphere. In cases where my association affects me negatively, I never get upset. Why? Because I practice *empathy*: I put myself in another person's shoes and try to see situations through their eyes. Practicing empathy allows us to acknowledge our neighbors' feelings. The habit of trying to imagine how others feel makes us human and mature.

Let me share a tool to help develop your sense of empathy:

1. Take a piece of paper. In the left column, write down a brief description of three situations in which someone wronged you. These could range from little hurts to deep wounds. Describe the errors and who committed them.

2.   In the right column, write down a brief description of three situations in which you wronged someone else. Specify the errors and the people you wronged.

Did this exercise help you recognize that you've wronged others in the same ways others have wronged you?

There will be friends in your life who choose not to associate with you publicly because they are not willing to take a stand. It doesn't mean these people are false friends. We all must take time to calculate the risk, knowing that associating our image with the wrong person or organization might cause us to lose something in the real world. Consider these questions:

+ What or who are you associated with (consciously or unconsciously)?
+ What have you been posting on your social media?

ASSOCIATIONS ARE EVERYWHERE

The theory of association is real, and it is possible, by your image associations, to make a stand without even knowing it. Let's look at some more examples of associations.

The organizations you support are associations. When you take a picture wearing a sports team's logo and post it to your social media, you won't gain much sympathy from those who cheer for a rival team.

The places you go and the events you attend are associations. Soccer players who are seen at parties every week gain the reputation of chasing women, drinking, and excess. Those who have never been caught in a situation like this maintain a public image of being "good guys."

During the COVID-19 pandemic, unusual things like wearing a mask in public or gathering with your family indoors during the holidays became associations. Choosing to cover (or not cover) half your face or to practice social distancing became akin to declaring your party lines.

When you associate with an aggressor, the one who was hurt by that person immediately sees you as a villain. Unfortunately, many people have been hurt by someone or an institution. I see this firsthand in my work all the time.

If my team posts a video on Instagram of me preaching in a church, I'll get a lot of views. But when I post a video of myself sharing the same content in a neutral environment, such as in a theater or a convention center, I'll get three or four times as many views. Why does this happen? Because many people have been hurt by the church. Others have not, but they have been scandalized by what they've seen on TV or by someone else's testimony. So, when my image is associated with the church, they disappear. It's as simple as that!

The theory of association can be difficult to navigate, but it also has its advantages. For instance, with technological advancements, it has become common for people to stream a live video on Instagram, YouTube, or Facebook with an influential guest. The idea is image association: the followers of one meet the followers of the other, and vice versa. Many people have won respect in the business world because of image association. After all, if that admired CEO posted a photo with so-and-so, he must be a good person who's skilled at what he does. That's how collective thinking works.

JOSEPH OF ARIMATHEA

Does the name Joseph of Arimathea ring a bell? Jesus had disciples and friends of every kind, including some secret admirers. Joseph of Arimathea was one of these, a secret disciple of Jesus. He wasn't one of Jesus's closest followers because he feared being seen in public with the Nazarene and having his image associated with Him. He wasn't a close friend, but he was strategic in the life of Christ and made history with a grand gesture after Jesus's death.

Joseph of Arimathea was a rich man. After Jesus was crucified, Joseph, driven by love, harnessed his influence to provide something Jesus needed: a burial place. He asked Pilate for Jesus's body so that he could offer Him a proper burial; his request granted, he placed Jesus's body in a new tomb that had been dug into a rock. (See John 19:38–42.) It seems like such a simple gesture, but it was from this tomb that Jesus rose from the dead three days later.

Q & A

Through my online course "Be an Expert on People," which has drawn thousands of participants, I receive countless questions. I would like to conclude each chapter in this book by answering one or two questions I've received that relate to the chapter's theme.

Q: Is there a way for a close friend to become a strategic friend? I was friends with a person for many years, but when I went through a critical moment, he didn't act with wisdom or love; instead, he abandoned and betrayed me. Should I keep him in my inner circle as a strategic friend or should I cut ties with him?

A: A person may move between the three spheres of friendship or even be expelled from them. Remember, you choose which people belong in each sphere based on their level of coexistence and trust. As for whether to relegate a friend to the strategic sphere or take him out of your spheres completely—it all depends on circumstances. Consider what is happening in your life right now and what circumstances you and your friend might face.

Q: Tiago, I have been cheated by people and have been bullied for as long as I can remember. I decided to stay away from people, preferring to be alone, but I've found this strategy is not doing me any good either. What do I have to do to have really close friends, then necessary and strategic ones?

A: Don't give up on people! Many people have hurt you, but others can contribute to your healing. Learning how to deal with different types of people will allow you to have happy relationships and feel more fulfilled. Give yourself a chance! If you don't, you will condemn yourself to being unhappy all the days of your life.

> "It is madness to hate all roses because you got scratched with one thorn."
> —Antoine de Saint-Exupéry

CONCLUSION

In the ideal world, there wouldn't be three spheres of friendship because all of us would be healthy friends with one another. However, in the real world, spheres are an excellent tool for protecting yourself and shielding yourself emotionally. Remember these key points:

- Although your **strategic friend** may be dear to you, your relationship has a functional purpose of benefiting you professionally or expanding your network.

- The **necessary friend** is one who is missing something for you emotionally. You need him to become a better person, whether emotionally or spiritually. Nevertheless, whether this person is a neighbor to share a barbecue with on Sundays, a relative to have a pizza with on Fridays, or a long-standing friend to go to the movies with on Saturdays, he or she is vital. We need these kinds of people in our lives.

- The **close friend** is a confidant who cares about you and your dreams. He loves you for you and not for what you represent or what you have to offer.

Are you ready to move forward?

A lot of knowledge awaits us ahead...let's go forward together!

2

UNAVOIDABLE ONES

People are disposable unless you want to be happy.

In the last chapter, we discussed how, in order to become an expert on people, you need to recognize who your friends are and what sphere of friendship they belong in. This determines the degree of trust and intimacy you should develop with them. The people and associations we discussed are in your life by choice. In this chapter, we'll be talking about the people you *have* to coexist with, even if you don't want to—people such as certain relatives, neighbors, and coworkers. I call the people in this category *unavoidable ones*. These people can be like a pebble in your shoe that makes your journey unpleasant. There are many different kinds of unavoidable people, and they come in different sizes and varieties. Since they vary so widely, we need to learn specific strategies for dealing with each type.

I can imagine your expression right now as you begin to mentally compile a list of the unavoidable people in your life. Some unavoidable people are so significant that they can't even be compared to a stone in your shoe; they're more like a boulder blocking your path. (Let me reassure you: in the next chapter I'll show you that there are people you *will* be able to avoid, the avoidable ones.)

As long as we're living in the real world, we are going to have to deal with people we'd rather avoid. Let's learn how to deal with them together.

UNAVOIDABLE ONES IN SCRIPTURE

You'll recall that the theories I present in this book are grounded in Scripture. The theory of the unavoidable ones is no exception. The Bible contains many emblematic examples of unavoidable people in various biblical characters' lives. Let's look at some examples to better understand this concept.

Consider David. Prior to becoming the king of Israel, David endured his brothers' mocking before he set out to face the Philistine giant Goliath on the battlefield. (See 1 Samuel 17.) After that, he was persecuted by his father-in-law, who sought to kill him several times.[4] Do you think this would have been easy to face? I can hardly imagine how painful it must have been! Yet he set his pain aside and became the greatest leader of the nation. What about you? How would you have reacted if you were David?

We also have Noah, the man who is known for saving humankind from the flood with his ark. He was exposed by his own son when he got drunk and stripped off his clothing. (See Genesis 9:20–29.) How would you move past this kind of humiliation?

Let's not forget Jacob, who had to flee because his brother Esau sought to kill him. Of course, Jacob was not an entirely innocent party. The family conflict began when Jacob "bought" his older brother Esau's birthright with a plate of food. Since this illegal purchase would only be made official through their father's blessing, Jacob then disguised himself as Esau by placing animal skins on his arms to mimic Esau's hairy arms. In this way he tricked his father Isaac, who was old and blind. (See Genesis 25, 27.) Believe it or not, years later, Jacob and Esau made peace with each other (see Genesis 33:1–17), but you can only imagine the trouble their feud caused in the interim.

---

4. Saul, king of Israel, offered his daughter to David in marriage even though he was already planning to kill him. Saul's invitation to be the king's son-in-law, along with David's flight, are recounted in 1 Samuel 18:17–31:7.

This wasn't the only time Jacob had problems with his family. His life was quite complicated! He was also cheated by his father-in-law in a marriage agreement and had to work for fourteen years, rather than the agreed-upon seven, to be able to marry Rachel. (See Genesis 29:15–30.)

And then there's Naomi, who, having suffered the loss of her two sons and husband, was abandoned by one of her daughters-in-law, Orpah, when she needed a companion the most. (See Ruth 1:1–14.)

Take a moment to read through these biblical accounts. As you do so, ask yourself: "What would I have done?" How would you have reacted in each of these situations?

AN UNAVOIDABLE REALITY

Unavoidable people represent a structure in our lives that we can't cancel or modify. One category of unavoidable people consists of our relatives: siblings, in-laws, parents, grandparents, uncles, aunts, and cousins, among others. People who are part of your work environment can also be considered unavoidable people.

The nature of these relationships doesn't change based on your decisions: you can't choose your mother, father, sister, or brother, and you can't change your boss unless you're willing to make some major career changes. It's impossible to simply ignore the unavoidable people in our lives, to pretend they don't exist. Instead, we must accept our reality and the role that unavoidability plays in our lives. I know it's not easy, but overcoming the denial phase is the first step in learning how to cope in the real world.

By now, you've probably identified a handful of people in your life who are a little bit difficult to deal with, who might qualify as unavoidable people. Perhaps you feel some resentment toward these people. Take a minute to make a list of the unavoidable people in your life who you've been struggling to deal with. Next, reflect on which strategies you have adopted (sometimes even unconsciously) to deal with the unavoidable people in your life. Have you ignored them? Have you confronted them? Finally—and this step is the most important one—take a minute to honestly consider what results you have obtained with these strategies. Have they brought you peace and comfort so that you have been able to deal with problems the best way you can?

What strategies do I use to deal with the unavoidable people in my life?	What results have I obtained? Am I being successful? Do I need to improve or find a more efficient and peace-promoting strategy?

DIRECT CONFRONTATION

Learning proper strategies for dealing with difficult people is vital because, as we'll see, not all strategies are equal. First, let's talk about direct confrontation. Is it a good option? The simple answer: no.

I'm sorry to inform you that if there is no room for constructive and outspoken dialogue, and if the parties involved lack maturity, it's not worth the effort—at least right away. Now, I'm not saying you should give up. In fact, I encourage the opposite: never give up. I'm simply suggesting you postpone. As the saying goes, what's the point of banging your head against a wall? You will only hurt yourself. Whoever starts a family fight will never win it. You may be in the right, but you'll lose too much emotionally.

> "There is only one way under high heaven to get the best of an argument—and that is to avoid it."
> —Dale Carnegie

As you're looking over your list, you might be saying, "Oh, Tiago, you have no idea what I've been through!" Well, I've been helping people in their relationships for thirteen years. I can't claim that I've seen everything, but I've seen a lot—enough that I'd be surprised if your story were 100 percent unique among the thousands I've heard.

Now, I am not trying to underestimate the story those names on your page represent and downplay the pain you have felt because of them. On the contrary! I have tremendous respect for the pain and experiences of each and every person who is reading this book. But my goal is to help you to gain perspective: if countless other people, all of whom have their own challenges and limitations, have managed to overcome their pain and resolve their difficult situations, then so can you. I'm confident that you, with your unique circumstances and capabilities, can successfully learn to cope with any person and situation that you encounter.

> "I am not what happened to me,
> I am what I choose to become."
> —Carl Jung

You cannot choose the wounds that are inflicted upon you, but you can decide how to react to them. You can't control how those unavoidable ones on your list will try to hurt you, but you can learn how to deal with each person and situation with intelligence and wisdom, in a way that promotes a peaceful outcome.

There are two approaches to life: one marked by happiness and the other by bitterness. There is no third option! The same is true for how you deal with unavoidable ones. Just remember, happiness and bitterness may be on the same road, but they take you to different destinations.

My goal is to encourage you to choose optimism in your relationships. Yet it is also important to set realistic expectations. I want you to understand that we aren't expecting miracles when it comes to unavoidable people; people aren't transformed overnight. We need to learn how to guard ourselves emotionally when we relate to these people. The first piece of armor we put on is to accept that a person is included among our unavoidable ones.

FAMILY MATTERS

It's time for the annual Christmas gathering, and there's that annoying brother-in-law. You can't stand being around him for even five minutes—you didn't choose him as a relative—and yet here you are, forced to spend time together year after year. He is an unavoidable person. He is a stone in your path, and you can't get around him and move on. He keeps standing right there. Your only choice is to learn how to deal with him. Every day of your life you have to submit to coexisting with him. Fighting against this will only thwart your happiness.

Any difficult relative in your life is, by definition, an unavoidable person because you had no choice but to be part of their family. Your father may have abandoned your family when you were a child, your mom may be cold and prickly, your sister may have slammed the door in your face, but all of them will keep on being who they are, biologically and emotionally speaking, no matter what choices you make.

It is worth noting that many of us enjoy positive, loving, life-giving relationships with our relatives. If you're one of these people, pause your reading and thank God for blessing you in this way. Unfortunately, millions of people are hindered by a problem you don't have, and their lifelong struggles with their relatives can be painful and exhausting. Others are just now finding themselves facing new conflicts brought on by a society that is increasingly polarized and eager to voice their opinions.

If you're someone whose relationships with relatives are marked by strife, then this section is for you. As you read it, keep this in mind: the key word when it comes to your relationships with unavoidable family members from now on is *forgiveness*.

TIME HEALS MOST WOUNDS

Let me tell you a story that took place in the city of São Paulo.

Doralice[5] was a twenty-one-year-old woman who was happy and healthy. She regularly engaged in social causes and was committed to contributing to her church's projects. She dreamed of being a teacher, getting married, and having three kids.

Dora took English lessons on Thursdays in a language school near downtown. After a while, she noticed a man always standing outside the school when she left class who seemed to be watching her. Although the man never

---

5. Name changed to preserve anonymity.

made an approach or talked to her, he made her feel uncomfortable and afraid. On the third week, when she spotted the man, she decided to call the police. At the police station later that night, she learned that the man who'd been watching her was her biological father.

Dora had no idea the father she'd known her whole life, Armando, wasn't her biological father. Armando, a dedicated and loving man, likewise had no clue that Dora was not his biological daughter. The whole family was surprised when Dora's mother, Gisele, confessed that, years before, she'd had an affair and decided to pretend that Dora was Armando's daughter.

Dear readers, no secret can be kept hidden forever! A little light is all it takes to make darkness fade away.

The family was left in shock. Gisele begged for their forgiveness. When she asked her ex-lover, "Why? Why? What are you doing here after so many years?" the man simply replied, "I'm getting old and didn't want to die without knowing my daughter."

When a TV talk-show host asked Dora if she would forgive her mom, she gave this answer: "Is there any other way of being happy? I'm going to spend some time alone and let time heal this pain." When it comes to family conflict, time is an effective painkiller.

We can learn a lot from Dora's response. If you can't solve a problem you're facing right now, just be quiet, pray, and wait. Try to develop self-control and distance yourself emotionally. But remember, our unavoidable people are bound to us. We can postpone dealing with them for a time, but, sooner or later, we will feel the need to be accepted.

> ## When it comes to family conflict, time is an effective painkiller.

RECONNECTION IN FORGIVENESS

Forgiveness doesn't mean endorsing the mistakes your relatives have made that have hurt you. Rather, it means releasing yourself from the pain of living life consumed by the things you've suffered. Forgiveness is not accepting someone's error as justifiable, but it is dropping from your shoulders the heavy load of resentment. To forgive is to free yourself from the pain someone else has caused you; it is refusing to let yourself drink the poison of offense.

Why do you think Joseph forgave his brothers when he was in the prime of his life in Egypt, when he was one of the most powerful guys in the world? He knew that it was not about being right or taking revenge; it wasn't about accepting what his brothers had done. It was a choice not to spoil everything, not to make life worse, not to lose the chance to be whole. Forgiveness is about reconnecting!

So, I ask you: Are you willing to forgive?

Forgiveness is a daily challenge, and one that no one else can undertake for you. It's an ability developed with effort, and it is the result of a decision. It's not some kind of overnight magic, but it is the best way to solve the problems we encounter with our "unavoidable ones." The premise of forgiveness is too important to be taken for granted.

THE POWER OF FORGIVENESS

The movie *Wonder*, based on the book of the same name by R. J. Palacio, tells the story of Auggie, a ten-year-old boy who was born with a rare facial deformity that required him to undergo twenty-seven surgeries to be able to breathe and see. He spent his childhood studying at home, and when he did go out, would dress up looking like an astronaut—helmet and all.

His parents decided it was time for him to start attending school when he reached the fifth grade, and this changed everything. Auggie had many challenges to face. The fantastic story of this boy is filled with many unavoidable people, including classmates who bullied him and a sister who felt neglected by her family because of the attention he got.

Wonder shows us the power of forgiveness as Auggie is betrayed by his best friend, Jack, and chooses to forgive him. Jack is so amazed by Auggie's decision to forgive him that he ends up helping Auggie demonstrate to the rest of their classmates that the most important thing about a person is what's on the inside.

People resist offering forgiveness because they have been hurt. What they don't realize is that forgiveness is the only way to break the emotional chains binding them and to build powerful relationships!

No one wants to live with pain, but if you refuse to let your arm be pricked by the needle delivering the medicine, you won't receive the cure. That's how it is with people.

> **No one wants to live with pain, but if you refuse to let your arm be pricked by the needle delivering the medicine, you won't receive the cure. That's how it is with people.**

The time to take quarrels to the grave is over!

DON'T GIVE UP

Just like you, I didn't choose my cousins or in-laws. I, too, have had serious problems with some of them. Yes, I've gotten angry. Yes, I've asked God to remove these people from my life. Yes, I've wanted to get revenge. Was courting these desires and negative thoughts worth it? No. Every week, when I showed up at my grandma's house, my unavoidable relatives were still there. The annual New Year's party only served to increase my anger!

It took me months to process some of the offenses and injustices committed against me. (Of course, in my view, I was right, but each person sees the situation their own way.) Finally, I realized I shouldn't keep allowing myself to get upset. Our life circumstances change only when we face them.

I eventually came to understand that people don't change just because I don't like them, and I realized that if I wanted to be happy and solve my problems with the unavoidable ones, I would have to start with myself.

In the ideal world, parents would love their kids and raise them well, and children would honor their parents. In the ideal world, relatives would coexist in harmony and peace, and people would help each other in their work environments and in the communities where they live. Remember, though: this world in which we live is not the ideal world, but the real one—and, as we've discussed, it is quite different from the ideal world. In this real world, many of us have been hurt, abandoned, and persecuted by those who were supposed to love and protect us.

Life is not a bed of roses; it is not piece of cake, as the popular sayings go. No, life is a rough sea we need to cross over in a little rowboat. But, as people say, "A smooth sea never made a skilled sailor." If you keep rowing, if you don't give up, you will reach dry land! Persistence is the key! Consider this ancient wisdom from Scripture:

If it is possible, as far as it depends on you, live at peace with everyone.

(Romans 12:18)

You may try the same strategy several times and have negative results. You may mind your own business and still get a negative result. You may try to please everyone (which, I should note, is impossible) and still get a negative result. Don't give up. You may need to try several strategies, but the key is to keep trying.

Problems are inevitable. There is no escape from them. The only thing you can do is keep facing them—and refuse to give up!

Let's close this line of thought with another verse from Scripture:

Anyone who does not provide for their relatives, and especially for their own household, has denied the faith and is worse than an unbeliever.

(1 Timothy 5:8)

LONGING FOR FAMILY

My studies on interpersonal relationships have led me to a very interesting conclusion: human beings have a desperate need to belong to a family—even if that family is far from perfect. Remember Jacob, whom we discussed earlier? When the opportunity to reconcile with his brother Esau after years of estrangement presented itself, Jacob prepared gifts and offerings and set out to meet him. To be accepted by Esau was more important than avenging the evil Esau had planned against Jacob in the past. (See Genesis 33:1–17.)

Our research team at Destiny Institute has worked with many people over the age of thirty who lacked parental records. These women and men had never met their fathers and had begun to search for them so that they could include their names on their birth certificates. They were not after money or heritage but identity.

One person we interviewed said, "I don't want anything other than to be somebody's child." Their search for the right to have a surname and a familial affiliation revealed the pain they had experienced at having been abandoned by their fathers.

People might try to run from the pain of being neglected or hurt by their parents, but the desire to be recognized will always be greater than emotional turmoil. Let's look at a few of these stories.

Janete, age thirty-four, was abandoned by her mom, who left her in the care of a neighbor. She grew up with a gaping hole left by her mother's absence. When Janete was thirty-one, she finally found her mother in another state. She bought a ticket and traveled there to surprise her. To her amazement, when she knocked on the door, her mom didn't even want to open it. She sent her back home. To this day, Janete tries to find a way to be accepted by her mom. Contempt hurts deeply, but Janete's desire to be recognized as her mother's daughter is greater than the open wound.

A person we will call Lucas had a very difficult childhood and adolescence. His father was a violent alcoholic and would regularly humiliate the family in public. Many times Lucas caught his mom having intimate relations with a neighbor while his father was at work. Believe me, this childhood was not easy to forget. When he turned eighteen, Lucas joined the army, and he saw his parents in the first row at his graduation ceremony. Despite his childhood difficulties, he smiled and thanked God that he was able to share that moment with his relatives.

These are only a few examples out of several stories we have been told.

Do you know what these people's stories teach me? That we all carry pain and frustration toward our unavoidable ones, but having them around—at a safe distance—is better than the alternative. Life already surprises us with irreparable losses. Why should we make it even worse?

HOW TO PURSUE PEACE

My organization Clube de Inteligência e Desenvolvimento (CID) has over six thousand students, and I daily receive hundreds of questions about relationships, including the following:

- "Tiago, what do I do with my coworker who loves competing with me and does whatever he can to get me into trouble? I didn't choose him as my coworker when I decided to accept this job."

- "Teacher, what do I do with the brother in faith with whom I hang out in church who envies all I have? It has become unbearable, but it doesn't feel right to move away from church only because a person bothers me."

- "My neighbor seems determined to dislike me. How do I go about reconciling with someone if I don't know what I've done wrong?"

These questions remind us, dear ones, that relatives aren't the only unavoidable people in our lives. There are many other categories of unavoidable ones we have to learn to coexist with: coworkers, fellow church members, members of the same social club, neighbors, and so on. In each of these cases, the person's continued existence in your life was not your choice. For instance, you may have chosen to take a certain job, but you didn't know that doing so would put you in daily contact with that difficult coworker. You may have chosen which house to buy, but you didn't choose who would live next door.

Life is a sequence of pitfalls and surprises. Flexibility and maturity are necessary tools to use when dealing with such unavoidable ones.

DEVELOP EMOTIONAL FLEXIBILITY

What is emotional flexibility? Let me explain this concept through a story.

When I moved to São Paulo, I lived in an apartment. As is typical in apartments, each resident was assigned a parking space. The parking spaces were clearly labeled. Yet my neighbor insisted on parking his car in my spot.

It wouldn't have been a big deal, except my space was clearly better. My neighbor's parking space had a pillar nearby that made it difficult to pull into, and it was right at the spot where the garage floor began to slant down toward the next level. My assigned spot, just one space over, was much more convenient.

I traveled often, and frequently I would pull into the garage late at night, exhausted after hours of flights, only to find his car parked in my spot. It would take me ten minutes to maneuver my car into a spot that wasn't mine. "This is so unfair! I have my rights!" I would grumble to myself.

Full of anger, I would brainstorm how to solve this annoyance. "I'll write a strongly worded letter," I would resolve, or "I'll knock at his door at three in the morning and give him a piece of my mind," or "I'll tell the landlord," or "I'll call the police." The ideas became increasingly drastic as my anger grew.

Negative feelings arise within us—that's normal. They become harmful when we allow them to master us. Fortunately, as someone dedicated to becoming a people specialist, I knew that the solution lay in *identifying* my negative emotions and promptly fighting against them with the right tools.

I held the key to banishing my neighbor's irritating behavior, and it lay not in my raging attitude but in my flexibility.

One Friday afternoon when I got home, I noticed my neighbor's car was dirty. I went to my apartment, changed my clothes, and returned to the parking garage with a bucket, soap, and rags. I washed his car, left it shining—and stuck a note on his windshield that read, "I noticed that you're parked in my spot. I know it's very hard to park in yours. If there is anything I can do to make your life easier, just let me know."

Dear readers, he not only stopped parking in my spot, but he became an ally in our condominium meetings.

Being flexible is the key to successful relationships. But it is more than that. Flexibility is a mental state. The American physicist Leonard Mlodinow emphasizes that flexible thinking leads us to generate and incorporate new ideas:

The capacity to let go of comfortable ideas;...the capability to rise above conventional mind-sets and to reframe the questions we ask; the ability to abandon our ingrained assumptions and open ourselves to new paradigms;...the willingness to experiment and be tolerant of failure. That's a diverse bouquet of talents…[that] have been revealed as different aspects of a coherent cognitive style. I call it elastic thinking. Elastic thinking is what endows us with the ability to solve novel problems and to overcome the neural and psychological barriers that can impede us from looking beyond the existing order.[6]

You can be as harsh and rigid as a pencil, but, remember, a pencil breaks more easily than rubber. Flexibility ensures durability. The more you are a dreamer, the more open-minded you are, the more flexible you will become in the face of other people's inflexibility.

> ## You can be as harsh and rigid as a pencil, but, remember, a pencil breaks more easily than rubber. Flexibility ensures durability.

If you fight against the disease of pride and allow yourself to become flexible, most of your problems will disappear. Consider this: to live up to your purpose in life, you will need peace, and you will need people to help you out. Don't negotiate away your peace, and don't create problems with people.

You only have one life. Do you want yours to be marked by warfare? I can't help but recall all those images of families crossing the Mediterranean Sea in perilous conditions to escape Syria. No one wants to live in a hostile environment. Take the necessary steps to make sure you aren't creating additional hostility in your life.

SPEAK WITH WISDOM

One day I posted this on my Twitter account: "I'm not able to say everything I think. And it's not out of insincerity, but wisdom." My post made people talk. The comments were replete with people recounting how they had lost friends, missed opportunities, and ruined relationships for failing to control their speech. A popular saying warns, "A closed mouth catches no flies." Expressing yourself in a way that maintains peace—and doesn't stir up

---

6. Leonard Mlodinow, *Elastic: Unlocking Your Brain's Ability to Embrace Change* (New York: Vintage Books, 2019), 5–6.

hostility—is an art. And as with all kinds of art, speaking with wisdom and clarity is something we must practice and develop.

Thomas Edison famously said, "Genius is 1 percent inspiration and 99 percent perspiration." Learning how to improve yourself and to control your tongue takes work, but given the alternative—getting into trouble—it is worth the effort. It's time to leave behind the teenager's way of thinking: "I don't take nonsense from anyone. It's tit for tat. That's the way I speak. Take it or leave it."

You won't get far in life if you don't grow in your relational maturity. Mastering the art of relationships with all people—including your unavoidable ones—is vital to success. It's impossible to succeed without engaging people. Even if you believe you're good enough alone, whatever your area of work, eventually you'll have to interact with people. Unless your goal in life is to become a hermit, you *have to* develop and maintain relationships.

FIND THE BALANCE

On a sunny Friday, one of those days meant to be full of life and joy and anticipation of the weekend, I woke up, ate breakfast, and checked my Facebook feed. I noticed a new post by someone I followed. As I read it, I began to feel nervous. I started muttering, "Who does this guy think he is? His post is just nonsense…ridiculous."

I kept thinking about that post as I went about my day. It wasn't until after I'd put myself together that I realized something was wrong *in me*. How can a stranger, a face on the Internet, spoil my Friday morning?

Being an expert on people doesn't make me a perfect person, but it does provide me with the ability to rapidly identify my negative feelings and behaviors and find the tools to adjust them. So I asked myself, "Tiago, why are you so bothered by this simple post? What has triggered this mix of difficult feelings? Do you envy or admire what this guy does?" It was at that point that I realized how imbalanced I was.

People who get you on your bad side are warning signs of how unbalanced you are.

Read that phrase again. When we're balanced, nothing can steal our peace. When we're emotionally balanced, nothing can capture our emotions.

PURSUE RECONCILIATION

I have struggled with attention deficit disorder my whole life. Occasionally I use medication to treat my symptoms. Without medication, a bird flying close to my window while I am writing is enough to steal my attention, and it can take almost an hour for me to refocus. In theory, the medicine helps me to maintain focus and become less distracted, allowing me to concentrate on my daily responsibilities.

One day, I woke up at eight o'clock, ready to tackle a busy schedule. I would have to go to the heliport in my building and get on a helicopter that would take me to the TV studio where I would take part in a recording session. Thinking through the steps alone was enough to make my head spin. I drank my coffee black, as I do every morning, and swallowed the pill my doctor had recommended.

As the day progressed, I began to feel off. I was feeling agitated, overcome by a strange mixture of feelings. When I arrived at the studio, I picked up the phone, overcome by joy, and started to call people. The problem is that they were people with whom I had lost touch.

For reasons we quite often don't remember, we leave people behind. We lose track of them. When we get upset by something they post, we block them on social media. Sadly, we give up on them.

That day, though—driven, unbeknownst to me, by the effects of the medicine I'd taken—I didn't hesitate to reach out. I called partners who had turned me away in the past, religious leaders who had spoken evil of me, friends who had ignored me when I had needed them the most. I called without hesitation, greeting them happily, enthusiastically wishing them a good morning.

I didn't feel any resentment or fear; I just made the call, no doubting or second-guessing. It was as if all my pride had left me.

Do you know what happened?

In that single morning, with the barrier of pride removed, I resumed friendships, approached people, valued those who were important in my life, and straightened out misunderstandings. Some of them I didn't speak to again after that morning, but I nevertheless felt like a weight had been taken off my shoulders.

The result? *Peace!*

So, you may ask me, "Tiago, is it worth it to reconnect with difficult people? Is it worth it to try to improve my relationships with my unavoidable ones?" To be honest, when I made those calls, I wasn't planning to become a lifelong friend of theirs again or have them over for dinner. However, the simple act of calling them took away the indifference that had somehow held my heart. Indifference kills more than cancer. Many people get sick because of hate directed at them from those they once admired or loved.

All it took was a call.

The next time I saw my doctor, I told him what had happened. "Doctor, this pill you gave me is strong, isn't it?" I asked.

"Why do you ask?" he said.

"Well, I got really excited fifteen minutes after taking it," I explained. "It seemed I had no shame or limits. I called a lot of people to say I loved them, and others I called asking for forgiveness. It was a bit embarrassing!"

He smiled and said the medicine does stir emotions a little and speeds thoughts, but it doesn't lead to changed attitudes. In other words, I'd been wanting to reach out and repair those relationships, but I hadn't had the courage to do it. For years, I'd been hindered by pride. The medicine took pride out of the equation.

How often do we ask those we love to stay away from us, when what we really need is a hug? How many times have we said we want to be alone, when what we really want is company? We are ashamed of admitting our weaknesses, of recognizing our limitations, and even of taking a positive step toward someone who has harmed us.

If you were to take medicine that would inhibit your loftiness, your self-ishness, your pride, your tendency to overthink or second-guess yourself, what would you do? Would you call someone? Would you try to reconcile an old hurt? Would you try to improve your interactions with the people you see on a day-to-day basis? If so, consider this book your medicine. Take a moment to get in touch with someone important to you.

JOSEPH OF EGYPT: PRIORITIZING PURPOSE

No one can bear betrayal. To be betrayed is to be defied. So imagine the pain of being sold by your own brothers simply out of jealousy! In this case, being sold means being forced to leave your father's house—to leave the comfort of your home, your favorite clothes, and your special breakfast—to go work as slave in a foreign land. That was what happened to Joseph, whose story we find in Genesis 37–47. When he was just a teenager, Joseph faced isolation as he was alone, enslaved, in a foreign country where everyone spoke a different language and had different cultural customs from those he was familiar with. Forced to work as a slave, he would have had limited sleep, limited food, and limited choices.

We can only imagine what feelings he had in the face of such injustice. Put yourself in Joseph's shoes. How would you deal with this pain, imagining your brothers laughing back home while you were suffering in a cell? Yes, a cell, because after he was sold, Joseph ended up imprisoned after he was unjustly accused. All this suffering because of envy!

The years passed for Joseph, and I imagine time seemed to go very slowly at first. Little by little, the wind of destiny started to blow favorably for Joseph. The divine conspiracy put him in the right place at the right time and with the right people.

After spending that critical period maturing, not complaining, Joseph developed the gifts, people skills, and demeanor to be among the greatest in the land, even as a slave. When Pharaoh faced an unsolvable problem, the king's butler, who had been in prison with Joseph, remembered that the Jewish young man had the gift of interpreting dreams and the wisdom to speak with strategic people. That was how God changed the luck of a former spoiled boy who became a slave: Joseph solved the riddle and was appointed governor of all Egypt.

When the whole earth entered a period of famine and all nations came to the new governor of Egypt to beg for food, they talked to Joseph. Thanks to Joseph's wisdom and his administrative gifts, Egypt alone still had food supplies.

And then came the greatest opportunity for revenge. Joseph's brothers—the same ones who had sold him years before—lined up to buy food. They had come from afar in an attempt to survive. They had no idea that the only source of food on earth was the same brother they had mistreated and discarded years before.

And then what?

The conclusion of this beautiful story is that Joseph, now all-powerful, recognized his brothers and, after testing them, took them to a private room, removed his royal clothes, and declared tearfully, *"I am your brother Joseph, the one you sold into Egypt!"* (Genesis 45:4).

His brothers were stunned by this news and overcome with fear. Then Joseph, the governor and manager of all the provisions in the land, said to them, *"Do not be distressed and do not be angry with yourselves for selling me here, because it was to save lives that God sent me ahead of you....So then, it was not you who sent me here, but God. He made me father to Pharaoh, lord of his entire household and ruler of all Egypt"* (Genesis 45:5, 8).

The purpose was bigger than the pain.

Joseph understood it. We understand it.

And so it will be with you!

Remember, whoever forgives last suffers more.

Life is like this: whoever forgives last suffers more.

Dealing with people may leave you wounded, but your future, your destiny, is more important than your present difficulties. Believe me!

Q & A

Q: Tiago, I can't forgive my father. He abandoned us for no reason. We experienced terrible hardship when I was young—hunger, the humiliation of not being able to pay our bills—because of his irresponsibility. Today he's been trying to reach out, but I don't respond. What should I do?

A: When the person who should protect us abandons us, our emotions fall apart. We lose direction. But, as I taught in this chapter, you can't pretend your father doesn't exist—and if you really weren't interested in resolving that relationship, you certainly wouldn't have written to me.

You want to reach a point of resolution, but you think that if you forgive your father, you will validate all the evil he caused you. But the truth is that whoever forgives feels free.

Many people who have lost their parents regret that they can no longer forgive their parents or receive forgiveness from them. My advice is that you forgive and be emotionally freed. You don't have to let your father become a part of your daily life, but you must realize that in your life, he will always have the emotional weight of being your father. To run away from this just spreads the pain.

I wish you peace and prosperity!

Q. Teacher, how do you deal with coworkers who envy you and gossip about you all the time, especially when one these people is your supervisor?

A: These kinds of unavoidable ones (coworkers and neighbors), unlike relatives who are eternal, may stay in our lives for a short time. You chose your work, but not those who were part of the "package." You wanted this position, but you didn't know who your supervisor would be. Now you have to deal with him!

My advice is to recognize that, if they envy you, it's because you're shining. This is a good sign. If they gossip, it's because the problem lies with them. What matters is that you don't gossip.

Get to know yourself so that their attitude doesn't change who you've been born to be. Be faithful to your values and role in this job. The good always triumphs over the bad, so have patience and choose the right side.

I assure you that, in the end, your achievements will silence your opponents.

Q. Some relatives I'm not close to insist on asking me tricky questions and are very nosy. For instance, they ask about my salary, if my love life is going well—they want to talk about my job and know everything about my life! How should I respond to them? Should I be straightforward and risk being rude by saying I don't want to talk about these subjects? How do I face these situations but avoid direct confrontation (as you recommend)?

A: You seem both smart and naïve. There's no way to withhold information from close relatives without causing embarrassment. Even if you don't see them as close, relatives tend to believe they should know everything about their family members. Whether they're driven by jealousy, envy, or curiosity, they will always ask.

My advice is simple: don't deny them information, only restrict them. It is tricky to outright avoid a question posed by an unavoidable one. On the other hand, if you answer their question—just not all the way—they will never really know it.

For instance, if they ask you, "How much do you earn?" you may reply, "Well, I'm glad to work at my company. We're appreciated, and the environment is creative." Consider offering a vague salary range, explaining that it depends on the person's education and work experience. Giving an overview without going into detail answers their question while protecting your privacy.

CONCLUSION

Unavoidable people clearly make our lives more difficult, yet there is a spiritual aspect to them in that we cannot choose who they are. God has made that decision for us. That is incredible!

Think about it: you chose your friend; God chose your father for you. You chose your spouse; God chose who your in-laws would be. You chose your business partner; God chose the coworkers you'd deal with day to day. All those people—your parents, your siblings, your in-laws, your coworkers—God chose them for you.

If we consider how we, as humans, can fail, but God is perfect—following this line of thinking—what relationships are more likely to be successful?

In some cases, perhaps the solution to dealing with our unavoidable ones lies in ourselves. After all, it's not easy to admit that our unavoidable ones can sometimes be the ones with a better attitude than ours. It's not easy to admit that our unavoidable ones can be better than us at some things (if not in many). It's not easy to admit that some of our unavoidable ones' errors are so hard to swallow because they're the same errors we see in ourselves and against which we fight. We're proud! We want to be the best at everything. Once we recognize that the issue is not always the other person, but sometimes ourselves, we can take steps to resolve it.

In the ideal world, we wouldn't have unavoidable people in our lives due to the simple fact that we all would be loving and truthful with each other. However, in the real world, it's impossible to deny that these people exist. So we're left with finding tools that help us to better deal with those we'd rather avoid. I believe we all can reach a point of peace in our relationships because I believe in people, even when they don't believe in themselves!

Collect moments and not things. But for this you will need people.

3

DEALING WITH AVOIDABLE ONES

Water teaches, with its wisdom,
that we can avoid obstacles
to reach the desired destination.
We don't need to clash;
we can bypass them!

Every day when you leave home, you will encounter people going about their daily activities. Some of these people you know; others are strangers. Some you meet regularly, like the cashier at the supermarket closest to your home; others you see rarely or just once, like your rideshare driver.

The people we encounter occasionally or just once in a lifetime are the *avoidable ones*. Very seldom will these people move from one sphere of friendship to another; rarely do you have time to develop any kind of deeper relationship with them. When it comes to the rideshare driver who brought you home from the airport last week, chances are rare that you will get the same driver again, let alone establish a friendship with him.

Like the unavoidable people we discussed in chapter 2, avoidable people come in many shapes and sizes. Some of them will smile at you; others will turn away their faces. Some of them won't like you; others will ask you questions about yourself. Some of them will ask you how your day is going; others—especially those passing through a difficult moment themselves—will ignore your remarks, no matter how open and sympathetic you are, and fail to reply. Our interactions with avoidable people are as varied as people themselves.

Unlike the unavoidable people we discussed in chapter 2, we are not obliged to coexist with avoidable people; we can avoid them. You may, for instance, change your hairdresser or dentist if you find yourself at odds with them. There are other people in town who can cut your hair or clean your teeth. These are not relationships you're obliged to keep working toward.

So why discuss them at all?

My goal in this book is to help you to learn how to deal with *all kinds of people*, from those you have known your whole life to those you know for just a moment. As you recognize the people in your life for who they are, you need to know how to deal with them in the best way you can. Let's go!

SHEEP AMONG WOLVES

When you leave home, you will encounter all sorts of people—kind and unkind, friendly and hostile. Life is just like this! In the ideal world, everyone would act gently with those around them. However, this is the real world, right? If you are aware of this reality ahead of time, you will suffer less. The simple fact of knowing this reality, even subconsciously, is already a kind of shielding. Knowledge shields us from the glances and words that try to hurt us.

Jesus knew that His followers would be navigating in the real world, so He warned us how we should act and react. Consider these words Jesus gave to His twelve disciples prior to sending them out to proclaim the good news of the kingdom of God: *"I am sending you out like sheep among wolves"* (Matthew 10:16).

We are sheep sent among wolves every day. Think about this: does a sheep fight a wolf?

Jesus the Master, after acknowledging the state of the world into which He was sending His followers, equipped them with instructions on how to act: *"Therefore be as shrewd as snakes and as innocent as doves"* (Matthew 10:16). Read that again: *"Be as **shrewd** as snakes and as **innocent** as doves."*

Have you observed how snakes behave?

In 2016 I was watching a series on serpents on the Discovery Channel and learned that a snake remains hidden, always waiting, ready to ambush. It doesn't face its enemies head-on, but it strikes when it deems it necessary, when it feels threatened. When it is in search of food, it is like a thief waiting for his victim to become distracted; the snake remains still and evaluates the right moment to strike.

Now think about how doves behave. Doves skitter across public squares, darting among the crowds. Without any pride, doves gorge on food people throw away or crumbs that fall to the ground. Sometimes you see them on the street, pecking away at something until a car approaches and they spread their wings and fly away. They're defined by simplicity!

When the Master advised His followers to be like doves, He was encouraging us to be simple and unpretentious, to depend on the care of others when necessary, and to have the wisdom to fly away when we are in danger. When He advised us to be like snakes, He was urging us to be cautious, to be strategic, to wait for the right time to act so that we might act and react in the best way possible.

FACILITATORS AND BLOCKERS

My speaking and teaching work requires me to travel extensively. Thus far, I've held trainings and in-person conferences on four continents. My extensive travel means that, every day, I deal with unknown people. Simply through experience, I've become something of an expert on the people you're bound to encounter at airports.

One time I arrived at the airport at the last minute to catch my flight. I ran to the check-in area with my passport and reservation and exclaimed to the airline attendant, relieved, "I made it! Whew! I'm on the three o'clock flight!"

The airline employee didn't even look up from shaping her nails as she said to me, "It's too late, sir. The flight is already closed."

Immediately I started to beg, "Please, I've got five minutes left before check-in is closed, and I have no luggage. Can you help me?"

She simply repeated, "Check-in is closed, sir!"

I grew desperate. This was the only flight to my destination that day. Another employee standing a few feet away at the same counter saw my despair and asked, "What's going on?"

I put on my best good-guy face and explained that I had no luggage and that, if I were to run, I would have time to get onto the plane before check-in was finished. She glanced at my passport and reservation, smiled, looked at her watch, and said, "Yes, if you run, there's still time. Take your boarding pass!"

I thanked her and ran—and, yes, I made my flight!

What was the difference between the two airline employees? One wanted to improve my chances of making my flight; the other wanted to block my path.

I hereby present to you the two kinds of avoidable people you will find wherever you go in your life: *facilitators* and *blockers*. Take a look at this chart to see what distinguishing features characterize these two groups:

Facilitators	Blockers
They are usually smiling.	They are usually ill-tempered.
They want to help even when the problem is not related to them.	They don't try to do good unless it helps them in some way.
They keep no record of wrongs.	They are embittered.
They care little about material gain.	They are miserly.
They are available and like to listen to others.	They are selfish.

From this chart, we can see that the attitudes of facilitators and blockers are diametrically opposed. There is one area, however, that I left off the chart: happiness. Those who are happy make other people's lives easier. They have no difficulty helping others and opening doors for people. They feel happy and content, and they want others to feel the same. On the other hand, those who feel sad and empty become blockers of other people's dreams, ideas, and joy. Even on sunny and happy days, amid parties, they end up disturbing somebody's life. Blockers are sad people.

Your emotional life, about which I speak in almost all of my previous books, is what determines the kind of person you are in your daily interactions. Your spiritual life is the fire that kindles your willingness to be better and help others. Your emotional life provides the balance for you to do this constantly.

THE GIRL WHO FACILITATED A MIRACLE

In one of my videos on YouTube, I tell a famous story from the Bible that conveys what it means to be a *facilitator*. This story, recounted in 2 Kings 5, tells of a little girl who has been kidnapped from her land, Jerusalem, by the Syrian army. After the people of Israel fell into the hands of this enemy nation, their holy city was destroyed and many Hebrews were taken as slaves. Among them was this girl.

Imagine how many dreams a child has. Can you even begin to understand all that was taken away from her? The love she would have received from her parents, the safety of living in her own home, the friends she had in her neighborhood—all this was abruptly interrupted by the Syrian army's destroying, killing, and kidnapping. The little girl became a slave in a foreign land.

These circumstances are frightening, aren't they? It's hard to consider such injustice!

However, as we read the text, we see that the girl doesn't seem too traumatized. On the contrary, when she realizes that her master, a Syrian general and war hero called Naaman, has leprosy, she sighs and says, *"If only my master would see the prophet who is in Samaria! He would cure him of his leprosy"* (2 Kings 5:3). She's speaking here of the famous prophet Elisha.

Wait a minute. Let me see if I got this right: this girl, who has had her future stolen and has suffered blatant injustice, informs her kidnapper of how he can solve his greatest problem? *Yes!*

Facilitators don't wait for the right time or opportune moment to do good. They simply do it! Each one gives what he or she has. As the Bible says, *"If anyone, then, knows the good they ought to do and doesn't do it, it is sin for them"* (James 4:17).

Folks, you're probably asking, "How can this be? What about *my* rights? What about the pain I feel? Are you saying it's easy to set my comfort aside for the sake of others?"

Do you think life was easy for the little girl in 2 Kings 5? Probably not. Nevertheless, it seems that she was more focused on solving the problems in front of her and going down in history (as she did) as a facilitator than on crying over her painful past and a life that no longer existed. This is what facilitators do. They focus on helping others when they can, without regard for personal gain.

How does the story end? Naaman, the Syrian commander, gains permission from the king of Israel to visit Elisha's house. The great prophet, through a messenger, commands Naaman to wash himself seven times on the Jordan River. Initially Naaman is upset that Elisha's proposed solution is so simple (take a bath, really?) and is offended that Elisha doesn't receive him personally. However, at his attendants' urging, Naaman decides to obey the man of God and is miraculously healed.

Are you ready to be a facilitator? Whose life can you make better today?

DEALING WITH BLOCKERS

There are people who will try to spoil your day simply because they are in a bad mood. (And unlike the little girl we just discussed, these people weren't even kidnapped as children and forced to work as slaves!) How many times have we entered a store where the salesperson, who is paid to help people, is not in the mood to be helpful? When this happens, we as customers tend to think, "Am I going to spend my money here? Am I really going to contribute to keeping this business running when the people paid to serve me promptly and attentively couldn't care less?"

Such people are *blockers*. Blockers are very common. We find them next to us in a traffic jam, in front of us at the convenience store, on the other side of the line on the phone, and even inside our own homes.

Let me tell you a story about a blocker. Many people who know me from the Internet have already heard this story. My post about it became known as the "Coffee at the airport" video, and it went viral on social media.

In 2015, Jeanine and I were at Galeão Airport in Rio de Janeiro, ready to embark on a trip to London. We stopped at an airport café to grab a coffee. I raised my hand to signal to the waiter that we needed her assistance. She took about ten minutes to approach our table, and when she finally arrived, she threw the menu (listing the café's exorbitantly priced drinks) on the table and left, clearly in a bad mood.

I was upset by her behavior; I wanted to get my coffee quickly and move to the departure lounge. My wife and I decided to order the cheapest coffee on the menu (which still cost more than we'd ever expected to spend on a cup of coffee!). With our decision made, I raised my hand again to summon the server to take my order. We waited another ten minutes. When she finally arrived at our table, she took note of our order with a frown and left without saying a single word. Several agonizing minutes later, she finally arrived with our coffee—but when she set down the tray, she did it so aggressively that the coffee sloshed over, and a quarter of that exorbitantly priced coffee spilled onto the saucer.

Jeanine, who is usually quiet tempered, got irritated and said, "Enough! Let's call the manager."

I kept calm and reminded Jeanine, "Darling, put yourself on her shoes. We're embarking to Europe, thank God, with money in our pockets. She's standing behind a counter. She arrived here at five in the morning and has been cleaning table after table. While she works, she sees everyone with their luggage embarking on their dream vacations and business projects. We don't know whether she left a sick child at home to come to work today; we have no idea if she was beaten by a violent husband this morning. We only see a disturbed (and apparently ill-mannered) person. But there must be something behind it. If we call the manager, we're going to ruin her day instead of save it."

At that time, I used a simple tool with this blocker. She wanted to spoil my day, intentionally or not, but I decided to make her day better.

I stood up, went to the counter, and asked for the bill. When she handed it to me, I held her hand and emphatically said, "Thank you!"

She bluntly replied, "Thanks for what?" and pulled her hand away.

I continued, "Thank you because, even with the problem you're facing—and I'm sure you're going through a very serious one—you still decided to leave home and serve people here. But I want to tell you that what you've been through is part of your journey, not your destination. Things are going to get better."

I left a tip and went on my way. As can be expected in a situation like this, she froze, taking in my words, and began to cry.

The name of the tool I used that day is *compassion*. Compassion is a powerful weapon. It is capable of disarming any blocker.

"But, Tiago, in practice, what is compassion all about?" you may ask.

Compassion is an evolution of empathy. Empathy is putting yourself in someone else's shoes; compassion is feeling what the other is feeling and not prioritizing yourself in a given situation. Do you understand?

> ### Compassion is the evolution of empathy.

APPROACHING RELATIONSHIPS WITH WISDOM AND MATURITY

It's interesting to reflect on this ancient piece of wisdom: *"A gentle answer turns away wrath, but a harsh word stirs up anger"* (Proverbs 15:1). What you say, the answer you give, the way you express yourself—all this can become the fuel that feeds an explosion or the extinguisher that puts out a fire.

> ### Your words are the fuel that feeds an explosion or the extinguisher that puts out a fire.

Having wisdom when you use words is an ancient solution to our contemporary problems.

"The great and truly wise man never says everything he thinks, but always thinks everything he says."
—Aristotle

The concept of speaking with wisdom is simple to understand but difficult to practice. Part of what makes choosing our words wisely such a challenge is the human characteristic that we call *impulse*.

Consider this scenario: a distracted child runs into the street in search of a toy. She doesn't look both ways and doesn't realize there is a car approaching at forty miles per hour. The driver's impulse is to brake when he spots the obstacle. In a few seconds, when the child realizes the danger and, paralyzed, looks at the driver with wide eyes, she finds that the driver has already passed her going four miles an hour and muttering to himself, "Where is the adult responsible for this child?"

The driver's impulse saved the child's life. However, if we reflect on this story further, we will also recognize that it was impulse that endangered the child in the first place. The child acted on impulse by running after the toy, thereby putting her life at risk, not realizing her error until it was too late. Certainly, she experienced three effects of her impulsive behavior: a racing heart, regret for her decision, and gratitude for the driver's skill.

You see, we all have a little of this child in us. Who of us has never trusted someone at first sight? We meet a person one day and immediately tell her our entire life story. We tell her our greatest weaknesses, trusting someone we didn't know existed until a few weeks ago. If we had waited two months, we would've known who that person really was. But it's already too late.

Impulsivity also drives what we say, the associations we make, and, of course, worst of all, our decisions. Being an impulsive person produces a lot of damage. We make promises we can't keep, we go where we shouldn't go, and we say things that we shouldn't even think, let alone speak out loud. Yet as time goes by and we experience setbacks caused by our own impulsivity (note that the other person is not to blame—you were the one who chose to trust someone you barely knew), maturity comes and helps us to master it.

The more mature you are—and maturity doesn't always depend on age—the more responsible and tolerant you become, and the less impulsive you will be. How do we become mature? I wish I could give you a simple answer. But if becoming a mature person were something quick and simple, there wouldn't be so many conflicts, wars, and diplomatic issues around the world. As I said, unfortunately, maturity doesn't necessarily come with age; it develops through understanding and accountability. So, you can start to mature…

+ if you decide to grow emotionally.

+ if you spend time with mature people, with the intention of learning from them.

+ if you read, study, and put into practice the subjects related to human coexistence.

+ if you read and meditate on the Bible and its principles, with the intention of obeying them.

+ if you learn to forgive.

+ if you overcome your greatest challenges and problems (which makes you grow).

+ if you seek to be humble.

+ if you are cautious and simple.

Some of these points are quite simple if you put them into practice, like those regarding studying and becoming knowledgeable on the topic. However, others require deeper engagement, like the search for humility and prudence. Your daily choices and your decision to put each one of these points into practice make the difference between merely desiring maturity and actually embracing it.

BAD DAYS

No matter how good of a person you are, you will inevitably have bad days. On those days, you act and react differently than you do on a normal day. We are human, and therefore we are vulnerable to external negative situations.

I remember one rainy day when I woke very early and started to pack my luggage for a trip in Brazil. Living in São Paulo at that time, I had to cross

Marginal Tietê to reach Guarulhos International Airport. We all know what happens in a big city when it rains: we were stuck in traffic for two hours and forty minutes amidst the rain and the chaos.

Since I already knew I was going to miss the flight, I started calling my office so they would get in touch with the staff of the event in the city I was going to. I spent time on the airline's app trying to get on the next flight; unfortunately, reading on my phone while the car was endlessly moving and stopping gave me a terrible headache.

To make things worse, Jeanine called me saying that Julia, our daughter, was not feeling well at school and that the principal had asked her to come right away and pick her up (it ended up being something minor, but it required a parent to be present nevertheless).

After all these problems, I arrived at the airport agitated, already regretting having left home that day. But then, on top of it all, the woman who attended me at the check-in counter made my life even harder. She began to tell me that I couldn't fly out that day because all the flights were overbooked, and so on.

At that very moment, someone tapped me on my shoulder and said, "Hi, Tiago! Can I take a picture with you?"

I looked at this woman and asked her, "Are you serious? Can't you see I'm in the middle of a problem here?"

The woman's hurt and offended expression let me know this wasn't my best moment. I wouldn't usually react this way—but I was having a bad day. I made the mistake of taking self-control and the people around me for granted. Thank God, I was able to reverse the situation. I went back to that lady, humbly apologized, and gave her due attention.

Having a bad day and getting upset about it is common. I'm grateful I had the wisdom that day to discern that the woman approaching me was not the cause of my problems. If I hadn't had the wisdom to discern this, or the ability to reverse the situation, I could have killed the admiration that woman had for me.

Poorly chosen words have a lot of power. Reconciliation is powerful too. Therefore, let's try not to make mistakes when we speak—but when we do, let's be ready to correct our mistake. And let us remember that the opposite also happens. Perhaps the person who spoke rudely to you today didn't do it to hurt you but only because he was having a bad day. Always have compassion when you consider other people's reactions.

> ## One day doesn't define who you are, but who you are defines your day.

Let me emphasize that we all make mistakes and will continue to make mistakes in one way or another in this life. One day doesn't define who you are, but who you are defines your day. When we make a mistake and are facing the consequences, we can reach for the tools of repentance and humility. Repentance allows us to recognize our mistake, and humility allows us to go to the person we have offended, apologize, and, if possible, fix our mistake.

Understand this: it's worth it!

How many wars and scandals throughout history could have been avoided if the party that had made a mistake had repented and humbly asked for forgiveness?

Human beings seem to like to complicate simple things in life!

Have you made a mistake? Ask for forgiveness.

Have you sinned? Repent.

> ## "An error in life is not a life of errors."
> ## —Father Zezinho

FACE YOUR PROBLEMS TODAY

In the romantic comedy *13 Going on 30*, teenager Jenna's dream is to get rid of some unavoidable people in her life—her schoolmates—so she doesn't have to deal with them anymore. She yearns for the popular group of girls at school to accept her and wants the affection of the most desirable boy in her grade. Hoping to buy her way into the group, she uses her intelligence to provide favors for them, but the results are fleeting.

Jenna wishes she could avoid this stage of life entirely and have a fulfilling life where she no longer needs to deal with those unavoidable people. (Who of us has never wished that?)

However, when she wakes up as a thirty-year-old, adult life doesn't seem as easy as she'd anticipated—especially when she has a successful carrier but the mind of a teenager! How sad she is when she realizes all she has left behind on her journey to "be accepted." She discovers she has lost essential things, like her value for justice and good relationships.

People are like this: in exchange for temporary acceptance, they replace the essential with the superficial. But, if we don't resolve our problems properly, our problems from the past will come back to haunt us.

Seeking forgiveness for our errors is something we should do every day!

Forgiveness is a vital medicine. Dr. Fred Luskin, a psychotherapist and researcher at Stanford University, and Carl Thoresen, who holds a PhD in psychology, developed a six-week study on forgiveness techniques. The results indicated that those who forgave others experienced reduced levels of stress, less anger, and had more trust that, in the future, they would forgive more and more easily. In addition, they saw improvements in physical symptoms such as chest and back pain, nausea, headaches, sleeplessness, and loss of appetite. Thus, Luskin concluded that forgiveness is a way to achieve calm and peace, both with others and with yourself.[7]

AVOID MAKING ENEMIES

In this book, one of my goals is to show you the *importance of not consciously making enemies*. You will naturally have a few enemies that you've made unintentionally; we all do. But don't set out to increase that number on purpose.

---

7. In his book, Luskin presents nine steps to forgiveness. See Fred Luskin, *Forgive for Good: A Proven Prescription for Health and Happiness* (San Francisco, CA: HarperOne, 2016).

Unfortunately, our culture seems dead-set on creating discord. We love arguments! There are even TV programs whose aim is to get people to argue with each other!

Is this fixation on arguing helping us? Not at all. More than 80 percent of the world's population is emotionally ill. This is a fact! Augusto Cury argues in his books that humanity is getting sick quickly and collectively.

According to a report published in the newspaper *The Guardian* in October 2018, ten out of forty illnesses in the world today have an emotional origin. Hair loss, ulcers, sleeplessness, and skin problems are some of the many psychosomatic symptoms that become physical in people's lives. The same report shows that the lack of programs available to help people tackle mid and long-term problems such as depression, panic attacks, and other syndromes will cost the global economy sixteen trillion dollars between 2010 and 2030.

Vikram Patel, a professor of medicine at Harvard University in Boston, is quoted in the article as predicting that the collective failure to respond to global psychological health crisis will result in a "monumental loss of human capabilities," and that one out of four people are already in a state of emotional panic.[8]

The COVID-19 pandemic only exacerbated the situation. Isolation, fear, and discord led to an increase in mental health problems like depression and anxiety among people of all ages. Mental health services are in greater demand than ever before.[9]

Dear reader, those who are experiencing so much emotional pressure that they're at risk of developing physical symptoms are not able to relate peacefully with those around them. Those who are struggling with complexes, anxiety, depression, and the like are not capable of getting along with others.

Remember that the difficult people who cross your path on a daily basis may be going through some of the problems mentioned above. This is one of

8. Sarah Boseley, "World in mental health crisis of 'monumental suffering,' say experts," *The Guardian*, October 9, 2018, https://www.theguardian.com/society/2018/oct/09/world-mental-health-crisis-monumental-suffering-say-experts.
9. "COVID-19 pandemic triggers 25% increase in prevalence of anxiety and depression worldwide," World Health Organization, March 2, 2022, https://www.who.int/news/item/02-03-2022-covid-19-pandemic-triggers-25-increase-in-prevalence-of-anxiety-and-depression-worldwide.

the reasons why dealing with people is so complex. Each person has his own story, his own intimate battles, his own emotional ghosts.

The book of ancient wisdom presents us with a solution for achieving happiness in such circumstances: *"Make sure that nobody pays back wrong for wrong"* (1 Thessalonians 5:15).

What can we conclude from this? You can't prevent people from harming you. You can't control what happens to you; external factors are involved. However, you alone can control how you react to harm; your reactions are internal.

Another verse from that wise, ancient text confirms that our interactions with others involve some level of individual and internal choice: *"If it is possible, as far as it depends on you, live at peace with everyone"* (Romans 12:18).

Negotiate with dollars or euros. Take a risk with bitcoin. But don't gamble with your peace! Nothing is more expensive than this. Putting it at risk is simply not worth it.

Reflect on your life and on the lives of those around you. What can anyone accomplish without peace?

> **Peace is only possible when the ability to forgive becomes greater than the desire to be right.**

There is an expression that became popular in Brazil, attributed to the poet Ferreira Gullar: "You have to choose whether you want to be happy or right!" In other words, remember that the real victory following an argument is not being right but having both parties walk away unscathed. Peace is only possible when the ability to forgive becomes greater than the desire to be right.

The sign of a victorious life is not the high number of friends we have but the low number of enemies we've made. It doesn't help to have ten friends if you have thirty enemies!

Pay special attention to the following excerpt. Highlight it, meditate on it, and share it with others. It is one of the most important pieces of advice you'll find in this book. This excerpt of wisdom, which has endured thousands of years, teaches us as follows:

> *The acts of the flesh are **obvious**: sexual immorality, impurity and debauchery; idolatry and witchcraft; **hatred**, **discord**, jealousy, **fits of rage**, selfish ambition, **dissensions**, factions and envy; drunkenness, orgies, and the like. I warn you, as I did before, that those who live like this **will not inherit** the kingdom of God.*   (Galatians 5:19–21)

Hatred, fits of rage, discord, dissensions, envy: all these little angers are in the same category as sins like prostitution, witchcraft, and even homicide. How much clearer could this be?

Don't feed animosity; resolve disagreements before it's too late.

Don't let the day end without resolving your anger.

Believe me, I wrote this book *to help you.*

Don't be excluded from the *greatest biblical promise* to human beings—the kingdom of God—because of enmity and hatred.

This is the moment! Don't delay. I'll wait. Pick up your phone and call, or at least text, those people with whom you need to make peace. Maybe you think there's nothing to apologize for because it was the other person who intended harm against you; if this is the case, consider this question: Do you want to be happy or be right? At this point, *to be happy* means to receive the promise of the kingdom of God. Would you rather receive the promise or to be right?

Notice that, in the book of ancient wisdom, Jesus also guides you to go to someone who has something against you and search for reconciliation: *"Therefore, if you…remember that your brother or sister has something against you…go and be reconciled to them"* (Matthew 5:23–24). Don't just settle for reconciliation when it is convenient for you; *actively seek it out.*

WE CHOOSE OUR WARS

When you create a problem on purpose, you've decided it's a war you're going to face. When you decide to continue an argument, you're voluntarily choosing to enter into a war. When someone harms you and you respond in any other way than showing them love, you've *opted* to be at war.

In the presence of war, there is the absence of peace.

In the presence of war, there is the absence of peace. I want to ask you something crucial: What price do you put on your peace? I can assure you that, in my life, peace is priceless!

Don't enter a war that is not yours. We all have enough problems in life; it's not sensible to get involved in somebody else's problems before you've solved your own issues. Being at peace is worth much more than that! It's worth much more than "picking up someone's else's fight," even if that person is very dear to you.

Understand that there's no such thing as an impartial report. When someone tells you something, their story is based on their own perception and skewed by the range of feelings that caused them to enter into the war in the first place. It's not your place to judge a disagreement that isn't even yours.

Pay attention to what divine wisdom says about serving as judge:

*Do not judge, or you too will be judged. For in the same **way** you judge others, you will be judged, and with the **measure** you use, it will be measured to you. Why do you look at the speck of sawdust in your brother's eye and pay no attention to the plank in your own eye? How can you say to your brother, "Let me take the speck out of your eye," when all the time there is a plank in your own eye? You **hypocrite**, first take the plank out of your own eye, and then you will see clearly to remove the speck from your brother's eye.* (Matthew 7:1–5)

ENEMIES OF HAPPINESS

I'm writing this chapter while visiting the city of Kuito in Angola, Africa. A civil war that lasted around thirty years greatly affected the beautiful and peaceful people living here. I can still see reflections of that violent time as I walk this city's streets: buildings riddled with bullet holes, houses destroyed, and a high percentage of people with amputations. One day I visited the city hospital to offer comfort in the form of hugs and prayers to those who were suffering. The experience was rich, but hard—sad, in fact.

I've learned a lot during my days here in Africa. For instance, I learned that in Bié, a province of Angola where many villagers are on the verge of starvation, people always reserve a handful of beans to pay the local sorcerer. They fear the local sorcerer because, according to legend, he has the power to paralyze people's lives. Yes, *to paralyze life*. Look, things don't have life; only people do. Spells are for *people*!

It's hard to fathom why the people in these regions would want to visit a sorcerer, isn't it? But I know the reason. It's envy.

It's almost impossible to believe that in villages where the people lack material resources, there is fervent envy. But it's true. It was during this trip that I came to understand that envy has nothing to do with money but everything to do with happiness.

People who are unhappy usually don't know how to deal with other people's happiness. The world in general is sad, and they are sad, so they simply can't accept that others are happy. Comparison between people generates dissatisfaction, which leads to different levels of envy. When people reach the highest level of envy, they become capable of taking food from their house, leaving their children to go hungry, so they can cast a spell against their envy.

PEOPLE, NOT THINGS

Have you seen the signs posted in big cities that say, "I'll bring back your loved ones within three days"? Well, when I see something like this, I think about how I've never seen a sign that says, "I'll bring you your dream car in three days" or "I'll find you the house of your dreams in three days." This is because *people*, not things, are the target of spells. People have emotions, and any "spiritual" activity needs emotions to be effective.

DEALING WITH ENVY

The Bible has a lot to say about envy (also called *jealousy*). Take a look at these well-known biblical passages:

+ *Anger is* **cruel** *and fury* **overwhelming***, but who can stand before* **jealousy***?* (Proverbs 27:4)

+ [Pilate] *knew it was out of **self-interest** that they had handed Jesus over to him.* (Matthew 27:18)
+ *Because the patriarchs **were jealous** of Joseph, they sold him as a slave into Egypt.* (Acts 7:9)

Recently I delivered a speech to more than three thousand women in São Paulo. I had lived in that city for four years, so I knew that the beautiful theater where I spoke usually hosted the most important events in the city; my speech was really popular.

I opened with a question: "How many times have you been envied?" Ninety-nine percent of the audience raised their hands and smiled.

Then I asked another question: "And how many of you have envied someone?" At this question, no one raised their hands.

"Folks, something is off here," I continued. Many laughed, and some blushed.

Envy is such a bad thing that everyone immediately understands when they have suffered by being its target. However, people are reluctant to confess when they are the one envying someone else.

Envy arises in two ways: it may come up naturally in someone, or it may be provoked. And when I say "provoked," I mean that you are the one stirring up envy in someone by showing off how happy you are. Therefore, if you can avoid showing off, you can avoid provoking a destructive feeling in others.

It is important to understand that envious people don't want to have something similar to what you have. They don't even want what you have (this would be greed). Rather, they want you to *lose* what you have because they don't have it. For instance, an envious woman doesn't want another woman's husband; she wants that other woman to lose her family, perhaps because she herself wasn't able to have a family or because she considers her own husband to be a dud.

There's no specific reason why someone envies you, but envy is usually tied to how happy you are.

I've seen millionaires envy their drivers simply because their drivers' children live in harmony, while the millionaires' fortunes are not enough to buy the love of their offspring.

The great Spanish writer José Luis Navajo warns us not to show off our happiness, comparing doing so to walking through a dangerous neighborhood decked out in our best jewels.

Here are three secrets for dealing with envy:

1.   Don't be a provocateur of envy.

2.   Pray to God and have biblical knowledge.

3.   When you're the subject of envy, respond with silence.

THE RISE OF INTERNET TROLLS

At this moment in history, in which we're experiencing a digital revolution, a generation of virtual haters has been born. The Internet has given voice to professionals who give opinions about other people's lives while they're sitting on their couch.

I myself have many critics and haters. As I look at haters' lives and attitudes, I can see they're usually unconsciously frustrated and emotionally ill people. Most of them create fake profiles to protect themselves, an emotional armor of sorts, with the goal of attacking people without getting caught. They know that if they are caught, they will be exposed and crushed.

Haters are just people who want to be who you are and do what you do. However, because they are sick, they create a world in which they can be a judge, judging and attacking people who do something relevant in their field. They are the so-called theologians who never studied at any university but correct your theology when, in their eyes, your biblical exposition is inadequate. People in their third marriage are always criticizing other people's relationships.

Haters distill their hatred on social media by pointing out other people's shortcomings, using profanity, and expressing unprovoked aggression. It takes some time to understand why something has been taken out of context and what lies behind these haters' aggression.

Flávio Augusto, one of the greatest Brazilian entrepreneurs of our time and owner of the Orlando City SC soccer team, posted on his social media a picture of a beautiful and harmless little dog with the caption, "This is Totó."

Next to this photo, he posted a picture of a mad dog, drooling and ready to attack, with the caption, "This is Totó with a cell phone in hand." Isn't this so true?

As people feel protected by being "anonymous" behind a cell phone screen, we see their true character and emotional sickness.

If you are ever a victim of internet haters, remember this: these people's problem lies within themselves and their unresolved past; you are not the problem! Don't get offended by their attitudes. They just want to get rid of the negative burden they carry, and they believe that cursing or criticizing someone publicly is an escape valve. Let these people live out their own drama; don't take their drama home and make it your own.

IGNORING HATERS

Not all haters are avoidable. For instance, your critic might be your father, a relative, or a coworker. In such cases, you'll need to use the tools I present throughout this book to find the best solution. However, many of us face haters who *are* avoidable—and we're not obliged to coexist with them. The strategy for dealing with such haters is simple: don't. Trust me, it's never worth it to respond to a critic or a hater.

> Trust me, it's never worth it to respond to a critic or a hater.

Avoidable haters or critics don't deserve your response because they are not searching for a solution or seeking a resolution. What they really want is your attention!

Recently a group of haters gathered to attack me simultaneously on social media. It was clearly an organized, coordinated attack. Hate speech (whereby, like people from the distant past, they were claiming to speak on God's behalf), cursing, and even threats were part of this attack. Instead of emotionally breaking down, I decided to study what was happening. It was incredible! I realized several things. First, I realized that all of them were trying to "correct" me, but none of them chose to do so privately, though they had the option to. They could have sent me a direct private message, but they clearly wanted to attack me in public.

Second, I noticed that they wouldn't attack me on their own social media; they didn't try to address their own audience; rather, they posted comments on my posts to offend me. This was so revealing! These haters weren't posting offensive comments for the purpose of improving me or even to prevent me from doing what I was doing; they were trying to gain exposure. They were trying to talk to my audience and ruin my image to gain some fame for themselves.

I noticed a third thing, as well. One of these haters said exactly this: "And this bastard is famous too." When I read this, I realized that some of the haters were motivated by envy. If I weren't a prominent figure, they would be on someone else's Instagram page cursing some other "celebrity."

When you're dealing with haters, remember these two things:

1. Jesus had more haters than you do.

2. Haters hate because they want your attention and your audience. *Never ever* respond to them. Your followers don't know your haters, but if you respond impulsively to your haters, you'll be giving them free publicity.

Ignoring haters is the best course forward. Remember, haters are like rocks on your path. There's no benefit to kicking a rock; you'll just hurt your foot.

> **Haters are like rocks on your path. There's no benefit to kicking a rock; you'll just hurt your foot.**

VALUE PEOPLE

Captain Charlie Plumb was a pilot during the Vietnam War. Today he's a sought-after motivational speaker in the United States. In his lectures, he tells a story titled "Who Packs Your Parachute?" and I'd like to share part of it with you. It happened this way:

After he had gone on many missions, Plumb's plane was shot down. Plumb survived thanks to a parachute, but he was nevertheless captured by the enemy and spent six years in a North Vietnamese prison.

After his release, when he returned to the United States, Plumb started to give lectures about his experience and what he had learned in prison. He recounts how, one day, at a restaurant, he was greeted by a man who smiled and said, "Hi, you're Charlie Plumb, the pilot whose plane was shot down in Vietnam, aren't you?"

"Yes. How did you know?" asked Plumb, amazed.

"I was the guy who would fold your parachute. It seems it worked, didn't it?"

Plumb was so surprised he nearly gasped. Gratefully, he replied, "It worked perfectly; otherwise, I wouldn't be here today. I owe my life to you!"

When he was alone later that night, Plumb had trouble sleeping. He kept thinking, "How many times must I have seen that man on the aircraft carrier, but did I ever say 'Good morning' to him? I was an arrogant pilot, and he was a simple sailor." He thought of the hours the sailor had spent humbly folding hundreds of parachutes, holding in his hands the lives of people he didn't even know.[10]

This story makes me wonder, who folded my parachutes today?

I'll conclude this chapter on avoidable people with one last piece of advice: value people.

Value people.

Value people, even if you don't know them or are not close to them. Some day they may be responsible for saving your life.

The person in front of you in line at the bank, whom you've never seen before, may at any moment have your life in his hands. Imagine this scenario, for instance: three robbers enter the bank, and they choose to use you as a human shield when the police arrive. No one has the remotest idea that the

---

10. To learn more, visit https://charlieplumb.com/.

man ahead of you in line is actually a plainclothes policeman. Seeing that you are in danger, this man steps in and neutralizes the robbers. You are now safe. Thank God you didn't offend that man before all this happened!

In life, you are known either by the problems you create or by those you solve. Choose to be part of the solution.

Q & A

Q: Tiago, I've been your follower for three months. During this time, I've learned so much about emotional life and spiritual principles. However, I must confess it is hard for me to control myself when a store clerk—someone who is paid to help customers—treats me badly. Is this normal, or am I the one who is emotionally sick?

A: It's normal to feel anger. The problem is when we have no control over our anger. Any emotion that masters us brings consequences we can't predict. Although it's the employee's mistake, since he is supposed to treat you well, you have to train yourself to react rationally, using your values as a starting point toward your attitude. Before you leave home, ask the Holy Spirit to guide you, ask for wisdom in your speech, and train your emotions to master whatever impulses you may have. And remember this: whoever masters your emotions masters you!

CONCLUSION

In the ideal world, avoidable people wouldn't exist because everyone would be emotionally healthy. In the real world, however, more and more people are not in control of their emotions and are going around unloading their frustrations on other people.

Therefore, understand this: it is *never* worth it to kick stones when we have the choice of walking around them.

Shall we continue?

> Your peace is too precious for you to waste it doing business with cheap people.

4

THE TWO IN ONE

"The wedding is where two people become one.
The marriage is where they decide which one."
—Robert Breault

"So they are no longer two, but one flesh."
—Matthew 19:6

Many people dream of living a beautiful love story; it seems that everybody wants to find love. We dream of loving and being loved; of living a life of partnership, fidelity, joy, and positive discovery. Having a happy ending in the style of "and they lived happily ever after" is the model we get from Hollywood movies and Disney cartoons. *However, those scripted happy endings are carefully constructed.*

The directors study a script written by a professional, choose a multidisciplinary team (cameramen, sound technicians, costume designers, makeup artists, cast, choreographers, etc.), develop an action plan, and then guide the actors to act out the scene in a precise way. The air-conditioning needs to be at the exact right temperature, and the lighting needs to be adequate and impeccable.

After the scene is captured, there is still the complex work of post-production. The sound design is carefully chosen to give the film that special touch, and, almost always, the melody is incredible and romantic, producing the necessary emotion for the *grand finale*. This is the only way to achieve the final result, the "happy ending."

Now think about it: if the scenes in movies are carefully constructed to produce a successful outcome, why do we think it is possible for us to have a happy ending in our own romantic lives without equal preparation?

For a marriage to be truly fulfilling and produce happiness for both spouses, you need to work hard to build perfect scenes, carefully choosing the environment, lines, script, and even the outfits.

In this chapter, I'll be introducing the two-in-one theory as well as the tools and practical concepts that will make this theory a reality in your life. Before you read further, however, you will first need to understand that the proper foundation for a successful marriage is understanding that marriage is not a supernatural encounter of twin souls who love each other naturally, who fit together perfectly and never disagree; rather, it is an ongoing building project. Marriage is a difficult promise two people make to live as if they were one. It's all about construction, not magic.

> ## Marriage is a difficult promise two people make to live as if they were one.

Do you know of any married couples who got married out of hatred? "I hate this guy, so I'm going to marry him"? No. Marriages like that simply don't exist. Everyone gets married out of love.

So, if *"love is as strong as death"* (Song of Songs 8:6), why do so many marriages die? And what do we make of the apostle Paul's words that love *"always protects, always trusts, always hopes, always perseveres"* (1 Corinthians 13:7)?

All relationships I've seen that ended at the halfway point (I say "halfway" because I believe marriage is meant to last until one spouse dies, so any rupture previous to that is "ending at the halfway point") fell apart when, at some point, the participants failed to observe the vital principles of the two-in-one theory.

In this chapter, we will examine each of these principles. However, before we continue, I need to issue a warning. If we were to go into each principle in depth, we would have enough material to fill several books. The goal of this chapter, therefore, is not to cover each principle exhaustively but to give a general overview of the principles and list basic ideas so that you will be able to:

+ determine which principle needs to be improved upon in your romantic relationship; and

+ determine *how* to improve in this principle by devoting yourself to studying books on each theme.

A WARNING: CHOOSE WISELY

When I was little, my mom would send me to the market to buy groceries for the week. She would give me a list along with tips and instructions, such as, "Open the egg carton you're planning to purchase and check each egg to make sure none is cracked"; "Look carefully at the garlic bulb to make sure no part of it is rotten."

Paying special attention to choosing quality ingredients is an essential step for ensuring you're putting a good meal on the table. Many people endure stomachaches because they are careless about the food they eat. Something rotten hidden in an otherwise beautiful piece of fruit can cause serious illness!

Now, think about it: how is it possible to have good judgment when we choose food and not when we select the person with whom we're going to spend our life?

Interestingly, most people are not careful when it comes to choosing their life partner. It is important to remember that being in love is not, in itself, a solid basis upon which to build a successful marriage. When passion fades away (and there are scientific studies proving that the state of passion is temporary), what is left? It is necessary to cultivate and nurture the relationship.

Choosing a partner carefully requires that you are able to discern which virtues you desire as well as which characteristics will bother you. If you fail to do so, you might find that coexistence with a hastily chosen partner will be unbearable.

As a pastor, I also encourage you to recognize that God may give you signs to show you if you're choosing the right person. I remember that right after I kissed Jeanine for the first time, I went back home and prayed, "Lord, she's the one. I want to marry her. I feel that it's she. If she also pleases You, give me a sign: let her move closer to my house." Two weeks later, the woman who would eventually become my mother-in-law called and asked me if I could drive her through the neighborhood on Saturday because they were thinking of moving there.

Divine signs are true, and they never go out of style!

THE FOUNDATIONAL PRINCIPLES OF THE TWO-IN-ONE THEORY

People sometimes take too long to realize that prevention is easier than finding a cure. The best way to avoid having a problematic marriage is to choose your partner well and ask for signs from heaven regarding your choice. Unfortunately, many times, we realize we didn't choose well only after we're already married. Is there a solution for these cases? Yes—as long as both spouses are fully committed to implementing all the foundational principles I'll be laying out.

Over the next few pages, I will be handing you a treasure map. Pay attention!

PRIORITIZING EACH OTHER

In the real world, knowing how to prioritize and respect the relationship you've decided to enter into is one of the most important foundations upon which to build the happy ending you've always dreamed of.

Consider this scenario: an obese person has decided to lose weight for her well-being and health. In order to maintain her health for her entire life, she will need to transform her mindset regarding food and physical exercise. If she holds on to the habits that led to her being obese in the first place, she may experience short-term results but will certainly gain the weight back as time goes by. She must implement lasting change from the inside out. Only then should she act on her choice to make a lifestyle change.

The same reasoning applies to marriage. You see, when I got married, it was not appropriate for me to keep the mentality—much less the habits—of a single person. My lifestyle needed to change, and that was a consequence of the choice I made to marry. When I chose to dedicate myself to my wife, all the elements and behaviors of my former, single life that would divert me from this purpose needed to be definitively erased. Do you understand?

Preventive reasoning is also necessary. This means abandoning any options along the way that would point to a future reality other than marital union. To act against marriage would be a kind of self-sabotage: you are essentially handing the ball to the opposing team when they're in the optimal position to score. If you don't want to lose the game, you should avoid any and every situation that gives the opposing team favorable conditions for scoring a goal.

The process of prioritizing isn't always easy. Consider this verse from Scripture:

That is why a man leaves his father and mother and is united to his wife.

(Genesis 2:24)

If, according to ancient wisdom, even a person's father and mother—those whom God commands us to honor—cease to be a priority compared to the commitment you've made to your spouse, imagine what priority we must place on other relationships! Adjusting the order of priority we assign to our friendships and other relationships can be tricky. However, it is vital that you preserve a mindset consistent with the choice you made to get married and that you prioritize everything that has to do with preserving your marital relationship.

I've noticed that selfishness and individualism are common characteristics among couples who come to me for help solving their relational problems. When someone decides to take on a lifestyle of two, instead of one, he should live for the other and not just for himself. I think this is not always clear to people who decide to bet on their future together. The cards are on the table, but you need to understand that the game you're playing isn't an individual one—it includes your partner. In a relationship, you will only have a good chance of winning if you play as a team. There's no point in doing everything yourself or discarding the contributions of the one person who stands to win or lose it all with you.

This doesn't mean that marriage requires you to lose your individuality and abandon your free will. However, it is important that you understand that, when you chose not to embark on the journey of life alone, you are now required to collaborate with your spouse in all things.

Occasionally, the pressure increases on your relationship, and a lot of nonsense can cross your mind. But, if you've chosen the right close friends, a good chat over a cup of coffee might be enough to release the stress and put your thoughts in order.

MAINTAINING FOCUS

Many athletes want to run like the Jamaican sprinter Usain Bolt. He is one of the fastest runners in the world, and many people who are passionate about sprinting study his techniques.

When Bolt is on the track, other athletes are there as well. Reporters and photographers are roaming around to record the race and interview the contestants (these people are true unavoidable ones!). There are people everywhere, people yelling in the stands; and, as we sometimes see, there are even rude people who throw bottles of water at the track to try to annoy the athletes.

Lots of things are going on around the track to tempt runners to lose their focus while they run. But amidst all this chaos, one thing we've *never* seen Usain Bolt do is look the other way. Bolt has developed quite an interesting technique: he addresses the fans and begins a kind of live choreography with the audience. In this way, he keeps the crowd united, strengthens his relationship with fans, forms a bond with the audience, and produces a favorable rhythm by which to run. He sets the scene to shine!

Married couples seeking to live by the two-in-one principle could learn a thing or two from Bolt—primarily this: it cannot be two in one if, in the race of life, you keep on looking the other way and getting distracted.

> ## It cannot be two in one if, in the race of life, you keep on looking the other way and getting distracted.

The two-in-one marriage is far beyond a hundred-meter sprint. It's a real marathon! Not getting distracted during the marriage marathon is one of many factors that contributes to the protection of your relationship, personal development, and longevity.

You must keep your focus. If you choose to get married, your focus from now on needs to be on a life of two. What's more, it's not enough to maintain focus for one day, one month, one year. No, your focus needs to be constant, every day. Otherwise, your relationship is destined to fail.

COMMITTING TO RECIPROCITY AND REPAIR

When I was a little boy, we would go to my maternal grandma's house for lunch some Sundays. Grandma Naná, as we used to call her, loved to cook for us. Although she and my grandpa Valdemar lived in the suburbs of Rio de Janeiro, they had a rural lifestyle. They had their own orchard full of fruit trees that grew guavas, mangos, and Pitanga fruit (also called Surinam cherries). They also had a chicken coop that helped set the country scene. The furniture and appliances in the house remained the same from my childhood until their deaths—even the fridge, the stove, and the TV. This only served to make their home seem even more rustic!

My grandpa used to say that we had to be friends with fix-it men, for we would always need their services. He had an account to which he would charge purchases at the butcher shop, but he would pay in cash for the technician's labor. He was from the generation of people who never threw away something they could use for the rest of their lives.

My grandpa's strategy for maintaining his house only worked because it was a two-way street. On the one side were those who wanted to fix their belongings; on the other side were those who knew how to fix them. Do you see what I mean?

Our generation is different in that it replaces items that no longer work properly instead of fixing them. Many factors contributed to this shift, of course: there are more options, more products available, different mindsets, and—at least it seems this way—things are no longer "made to last," as they used to be. All this has reinforced the idea that replacing is a good substitute for repairing.

What we must consider, however, is whether happiness is found in getting something new or in seeking to successfully finish what you have already started. Let me ask you something: is an athlete's success found in finishing the race he started or in giving up in the middle of it to start another race?

Both people engaged in a two-in-one relationship have to *want* to fix things. Are you both committed to making the necessary repairs to make your two-way relationship work? Reciprocity in this regard is absolutely essential. When only one of the two people involved is committed, the path of this relationship will promise much suffering.

When only one person loves, when only one person respects the rules of the game—in these cases, it is almost impossible to keep the covenant.

SURRENDERING

Why do extramarital affairs keep happening even though they require secrecy, invite danger, and are nearly universally frowned upon? They keep happening because the lovers act as one and are determined to make the affair work! Both participants are completely united in a single desire, have a single motivation, and have reached level 10 surrender. I've seen this so many times over my years of helping people who have been involved in extramarital relationships. It is a pity they used their highest level of surrender on something that causes them long-term harm instead of using it to strengthen the commitment they've already made.

The real world is a good benchmark and target in this case. Everyone who has found success—whether in business, sports, finances, or family—has shown the highest level of surrender. I'm convinced that luck doesn't exist. What exists is dedication and personal surrender to make it work.

Stop and reflect on your life now. Be honest with yourself. On a scale of 0 to 10, what is your level of surrender to your two-in-one relationship? What is your spouse's level?

Believe me, a couple's level of surrender to their relationship determines whether they will win or lose as a couple. The good news is that this is a conscious decision; that is, if both of you are willing, you can consciously increase your level of surrender. The key to doing so together is dialogue.

How? From the essential alignments, which are the next foundational principle we'll discuss.

MAINTAINING ESSENTIAL ALIGNMENTS

How can two people be happy living together as a married couple if they come from vastly different backgrounds? Consider how your relationship would be affected if...

+ one of you was starved as a child, while the other was a well-fed.

+ one of you studied at the best schools, while the other didn't even finish elementary school.

+ one of you was raised by both a father and mother, and the other was abandoned by his parents.

+ one of you has faith that can move mountains, while the other doesn't believe in anything.

We need to understand that different backgrounds and values generate opposing views about the future. In life everything is risky, but failing to align in your relationship with another person is risking too much.

> In life everything is risky, but failing to align in your relationship with another person is risking too much.

When you are building a two-in-one life, you need to understand and identify *general* and *specific* requirements. General requirements are requirements that everyone expects, a collective concordance, a social paradigm. Fidelity, for instance, is a general requirement. Specific requirements are the set of things that are important to each spouse; these vary according to background, past frustrations, future expectations, and so on.

For example, let's look at the notion of fidelity. Regardless of your general understanding of the concept, you are bound to have your own ideas of how fidelity is either maintained or broken. For instance, upon discovering that her husband spent the whole night at dinner talking with and confiding secrets to another woman, a wife may feel betrayed. Her understanding of fidelity extends beyond physical boundaries to encompass her emotional life, as well.

Therefore, it is vital to understand a concept beyond its general meaning; you also have to understand what your partner regards as specific rules around that general concept. Let's look at some other examples:

GENERAL RULES VERSUS SPECIFIC RULES

CONCEPT	GENERAL SCOPE	SPECIFIC SCOPE
Fidelity	Refraining from having physical relationships with other people	Not flirting with people on social media; keeping a healthy distance from people of the opposite sex; always acting as if your spouse were present
Complicity	Supporting your partner's dreams and projects	Not doing anything in private; not exposing each other's secrets; never speaking ill of one another to other people
Respect	Showing your partner consideration	Never making your partner feel like they are talking to themselves; not uttering negative words or offenses; leaving behind your parents and fully taking on the role of married spouse

CONCEPT	GENERAL SCOPE	SPECIFIC SCOPE
Integrity	Practicing honesty	Always paying the bills on time; honoring every commitment you've made
Affection	Physically or verbally demonstrating fondness	Washing the dishes; taking out the garbage; leaving a thoughtful note; giving a foot massage; listening; asking your spouse out on a date

> A couple should talk about their basic values and dialogue about their perspectives on general rules and specific rules.

What makes one person in the relationship feel loved and respected is not necessarily the same thing that makes the other person feel this way. People are different! As such, couples should work out a strategy to respect each other's personalities and points of view, and determine and define the general and specific rules of their marriage. This will prevent many exhausting discussions and will bring them closer together.

START TALKING!

In the movie *The Boy Who Harnessed the Wind*, there is a scene that made me laugh and cry at the same time. The main character, a boy named William, was known for fixing broken radios and cassette decks with very few resources. One day, he was on his roof fixing a leak when his neighbor and client arrived to inquire whether William had yet fixed his radio. "William, where's my radio?" he asked.

"Mr. Bamusi, please, just a few more days. I'm finding the problem," replied the boy.

The man groaned in frustration and muttered, "He's forcing me to come back from work and talk to my wife and children."

People are like this: they get married out of passion and then stop investing in the relationship; after that, just talking to each other becomes a burden!

It is true, talking can be a difficult and tiring task between two people. But to become one, a couple needs to dedicate to each other the most precious thing they have: time.[11] And the time should be *quality time*—time that is truly dedicated to each other. The best way to spend quality time is by talking! Talk, listen, and be listened to; be aware of and willing to listen to each other.

The exhaustion of a week of work, the wounds of the past, the lack of time in the present, the expectations of the future—all these burdens and more become easier to bear after a good chat. Without this much-needed link, the people we meet throughout our day start to look more interesting than those we find at home. Our mind becomes addicted to external pleasures, and we easily forget what we struggled so hard to have.

Talking can be a difficult and tiring task between two people.

Marriage is one of the most important relationships—if not *the most important* relationship—in your life and is directly related to your short-term and long-term happiness. It is worthy of your energy and time! Keeping love alive requires intention and dedication. Therefore, overcome your barriers, your pride, and your laziness as you fight for your marriage. Be patient, have discernment, and start talking to each other!

Jesus describes marriage in this way, quoting from the book of Genesis:

---

11. I discuss this in greater detail in my book *O maior poder do mundo* [*The Greatest Power in the World*], (São Paulo: Editora Vida, 2021).

And the two will become one flesh. So they are no longer two, but one flesh. (Mark 10:8)

To turn two stories into one is not an easy or quick task. However, according to ancient biblical wisdom, it is possible. The big question is, how? The only natural way I know of turning two into one is through the birth of a child. Both the paternal and maternal DNA and genes are present in a child: the mother's eyes, the father's hair, the mannerisms of the mother, the temper of the father. But if we think about the couple's daily life, how do two become one? They need to be aligned in their expectations, ideologies, agenda, and lifestyle. Let's take a closer look at each of these aspects.

EXPECTATIONS

One of the main mistakes married people make is to hold different expectations about their relationship and their future. Frustrations are inevitable when your expectations are out of alignment. What do you expect from your life together? Where do you hope to arrive? What is vital in order for your relationship to be considered successful? What makes you happy? Talk about your expectations as soon as possible and as regularly as possible to make sure you're on the same path.

IDEOLOGIES

In our world today, we're divided by ideologies: right or left, LGBTQ+ or the traditional family, pro-guns or anti-violence, Calvinism or Arminianism. Politics, religion, and other cultural factors have separated people—including spouses. Aligning your ideologies is really very important in the two-in-one life.

I had the privilege of marrying Jeanine when we were both fairly young. As a result, we basically developed our mindsets together. We think similarly about many things in life, caring about the same things and feeling indifferent about the same things. We think so alike in terms of our ideologies that sometimes it makes us laugh.

Some people, however, meet their spouse much later in life, when they are more settled in their ways and beliefs. For such couples, aligning ideologies can be more challenging. However, it is worth the effort.

Things like politics and theology can be divisive. I won't claim that any one political or theological viewpoint is the right one; however, if possible, couples should stay on the same side as each other—or take no side at all. That way, wherever they fall on the spectrum, they will be there together.

AGENDA

The two-in-one agenda must be unique. When I say "agenda," I'm not referring to the daily schedule, nor to professional objectives, but to a life agenda: your goals and objectives.

Consider what would happen if, when asked, "Where do you see yourself in five years?" a husband replied, "In five years, I want to be living in England and to have finished my master's degree," to which his wife responded, "Are you kidding?" Does this couple have any chance of succeeding? Very little!

Jeanine has her own appointments during the day. She has her monthly schedule of meetings at our children's school, work commitments, and personal care days (e.g., going to the beauty parlor, spa, and so on). My work schedule and my monthly appointments are totally different from hers, but our life agenda is aligned. We plan the future together; we dream of the coming years side by side.

Couples can keep their own day-to-day agendas, but when it comes to their future together, their agendas must be aligned.

LIFESTYLE

A woman committed to physical fitness is married to a glutton. An adventurer is married to a homebody. A party girl is married to a family man. The popular saying tells us that opposites attract, but completely different lifestyles can cause more disruption than attraction.

I love traveling and getting to know new places and cultures. Whenever I have some time on my agenda, I find a way to go to a foreign city and learn something new. When Jeanine and I travel together, our rhythm is identical. We have developed similar styles and similar tastes. Of course, we diverge in some things, but I think the years we've lived together have made us want the same things. We want to sleep in, have an excellent breakfast—whether at the hotel or at the best café in town—walk through one or two places in the morning, then eat lunch at a restaurant we've preselected on the Internet or that was recommended by a friend. In the afternoon, we take a little rest, and around five in the afternoon we enjoy a good coffee.

We slow down our pace when we're on vacation, but when we are at home, at the end of a busy and frantic day, we like to eat together at the table while we talk about life.

Having your lifestyle in alignment will help you avoid stones on the road. After all, *we don't stumble over mountains but on pebbles.*

ENEMIES OF MARRIAGE

In the Hollywood movies and Disney cartoons I mentioned at the beginning of this chapter, there is always an enemy on the prowl. Marriages have enemies too, and in marriage, as in movies, it is not always easy to identify the enemy if we aren't paying close attention. The archenemies of the two-in-one marriage can cause a marriage to fail if we let them. If you are committed to making your marriage work and don't want to leave things to chance, be very careful regarding the following:

+ Secrets

+ Comparison

+ Communication

+ Discipline

+ Physical intimacy

+ Money

Let's explore each of these potential hazards further.

SECRETS

In a two-in-one covenant, you can't have secrets. I know this is a delicate matter, but in the real world, secrets kill deals and promises. One spouse may feel betrayed when they discover the other spouse's secret, and this can kill the relationship. Trust is a key element for success in marriage, and once it is broken, it's the most difficult thing to restore.

The bank password, okay; the cell phone password, no way!

Since Jeanine and I started our life together at a young age, we didn't have many dilemmas. Jeanine was just under eighteen years old when we got married, and I was in my mid-twenties. We knew nothing about life; we learned everything together.

My father, who was a soldier and a pastor, had taught me to honor the pacts I made, especially the most important of them all: marriage. I decided to live without having anything to hide. Believe me, in the ideal world it's simple to be transparent. In the real world, it's difficult and embarrassing. To bring to light what has been in darkness is painful. However, this is the only way of keeping the covenant.

Human beings are not perfect. We are all in the wrong at some point. That's why Jesus forgave us first, so that we could follow His example and learn how to forgive, too. I believe that the greatest sin is not to be in the wrong but to hide wrongdoing.

Avoid keeping secrets. The bank password, okay; the cell phone password, no way! This is so important that I could write another book on this single subject.

COMPARISON

Comparing yourself to others is a grand strategy for becoming a sad and unhappy person. If you want to be depressed, just compare your car with your neighbor's car, your house with your friend's house, your job with your brother's job, or your physique with the physique of a social media influencer.

It's inevitable to make one comparison or another. It becomes a problem when you spend your life measuring yourself according to others. This type of behavior will certainly destroy your two-in-one covenant.

You cannot measure your marriage by another couple's reality—*ever*.

Each couple has their own story, and most people never expose their problems publicly. Those "perfect" couples on Instagram show you only what they decide to post, not their daily truth. Even when they post about their sorrows, we're still seeing only a fraction of their life. Social media is not real life. You might even say that your Facebook wall is for sharing good times—for the hard times, there is the Wailing Wall.

COMMUNICATION

We once welcomed a very special couple into our home. We were on the verge of closing a great deal with their company, and we had prepared a dinner to strengthen our friendship. We shared laughter and great conversation for two hours. After finishing a farewell coffee, we closed the door behind them, and I looked at Jeanine and said, "This guy is *too* rich. Have you heard he has a private jet? He received a worldwide prize for I don't know what."

Jeanine smiled as if she hadn't heard my comment and said, "I recommended our dermatologist to his wife. She has very sensitive skin."

Conclusion: same scene, completely different perceptions.

We need to understand that, often, men and women have different ways of thinking. A man usually pays attention to status. A man will rarely say something like, "The guy was a little bald" after he meets someone. What you might hear him say instead are comments like the following:

+ "Have you seen so-and-so's car?"

+ "He is director of a multinational corporation!"

+ "He has an account at that investment bank."

+ "I don't even believe it, but he's friend with that guy."

+ "Gosh, he goes to work by helicopter on Fridays."

Women, on the other hand, often pay attention to aesthetics. You might hear them say things like:

+ "Did you see that skin, girl?"

+ "She's carrying a Chanel handbag, wow!"

+ "How does she manage to stay so thin?"

+ "What about that hair?"[12]

To be clear, I don't want to generalize. It's obvious that both men and women may deviate from this general rule. However, I am trying to highlight

---

12. Thanks to my wife, Jeanine, for these examples.

the idea so beautifully expressed in the classic book *Men Are from Mars, Women Are from Venus*.[13]

Frequently when I am working with couples in crisis, I find some of the same problems. The woman expects her husband to guess her thoughts and desires. The man complains that he does everything in their marriage. The woman has a sullen expression and insists that there's nothing wrong, when this is obviously a lie.

When we begin to understand that men and women live in different worlds, we start to take some steps toward victory; we understand that our spouse might not understand that he or she is leaving a lot to be desired (and that the opposite might also be true). Everyone has shortcomings. We can't expect our life partner to be perfect. Maturity in expectations and communication is an important factor for those in a two-in-one relationship.

> ### Everyone has shortcomings.
> ### Don't expect your life partner to be perfect.

DISCIPLINE

There are so many tasty foods in this life, but most of the foods that give us pleasure also contribute to weight gain and negatively affect our health. I love pizza and cheeseburgers, and I have a hard time turning down ice cream for dessert. However, if I gave in every time I craved these foods, my waistline would expand as my blood sugar levels rose.

We've seen that focusing on one thing means being able to say no to everything else. Discipline is staying focused every day on the two-in-one life.

Life is like a fork in the road: you have to decide whether to turn right or left. You can't go both ways at the same time, and you will only reach your final destination if you go all the way. Discipline is the tool that guarantees you will get where you want to go. Whoever lives without discipline dies without dignity.

---

13. John Gray, *Men Are from Mars, Women Are from Venus: The Classic Guide to Understanding the Opposite Sex* (New York: HarperCollins Publishers, 1992).

Whoever lives without discipline dies without dignity.

PHYSICAL INTIMACY

Around 60 percent of men who come to me for help because they are dissatisfied in their marriage report problems with sexual intimacy.

Men want sex but are not patient, and sometimes they lack skill in this matter. Women generally don't desire sex as much as men do; they require emotional rather than physical engagement.

Sexual intimacy is a blazing fire that keeps the relationship warm. A problematic or unsatisfactory sex life will ruin a marriage sooner or later. It is important to understand that mutual sexual satisfaction is not automatic or guaranteed, and both of you should address this issue as a matter of priority. No matter how embarrassing it may seem at first, couples will have to talk openly about sex if they want to live well.

Many couples struggle in their sex life because they lack discipline when it comes to eating and exercising, and the lack of flexibility, physical fitness, and willingness makes everything more difficult. There are also those who let the routine, the lack of time, and the job of caring for their children compromise their commitment to keeping their intimate life hot.

Others lack moral discipline and are addicted to virtual pleasures. For them, real sex is boring and dull. Some men, because of excessive pornography, literally prefer masturbating in the bathroom to going to their wives who are available in the bedroom. What a sad reality!

Whatever your reality is, be aware that sex is an experience of complex connection—a union of body, soul, and spirit—that represents the height of intimacy. Embracing this union fully unites and strengthens couples. Talk with your spouse about your physical relationship and seek counseling in this area if you need it. Go see a doctor if there is any hint that something is wrong. It's worth it!

MONEY

Planning is essential when it comes to dealing with your finances as a couple. From the moment you become two-in-one, it's no longer "your money" or "my money." It's "our money."

As such, you will need to openly discuss topics that, for some, may be delicate: how much each one of you earns, what your expenses will be, and what you priorities will be from now on. It's beneficial to determine who will be in charge of your finances, who will be responsible for paying the bills, and how you will make financial decisions.

For instance, in my home, I'm responsible for bringing in 90 percent of our income. Jeanine contributes with income from her online store. However, she's the one who manages our finances. She takes care of the bills as well as our banking. We decide together how we will invest for the future.

Who does what financially as a couple really matters.

If you need help in this area, don't hesitate to seek training on the matter to keep control of your money. A serious financial crisis can undermine even the strongest of marriages.

GETTING HELP

During one of my live broadcasts on Instagram, a woman said to me, "Tiago, I've been married for thirty years and I don't know how much my husband makes or what his cell phone password is. He never consults me when he makes a decision. What should I do?"

I replied, "Thirty years have passed, and you're just now looking for help? Well, better late than never."

It's very important to remember that, if you find you're unable to solve an issue in your marriage alone, you should not hesitate to ask for help. Don't wait until you're already drowning to put on your life jacket.

In that wonderful, ideal world we keep talking about, couples love each other passionately. Their love is founded on fidelity and partnership. The father cares for his children well and provides for the family. The mother, always teaching, is kind and happy and keeps the home in balance.

However, in the real world, with all its injustice, the husband, who promised at the altar "to have and to hold, from this day forward, for better or for worse, for richer or for poorer, in sickness and in health, until death do us part," is now distracted with a "fella" at work or holding secret text conversations and viewing pornography. At the slightest sign of disagreement, he threatens to leave the house, thus allowing insecurity to rule over a home that should be a safe haven. As for the kids, they—unlike kids in those perfect-world-TV-commercials—are disobedient and are causing serious problems. The wife, already tired and frustrated with her reality, starts brainstorming escape routes.

Accepting that your life is not perfect and that living as a couple has been a huge burden may be the beginning of change, a true 180-degree turning point. On the other hand, pretending that everything will improve on its own, out of the blue, and never asking for help will inevitably lead to a failed relationship.

Let me repeat—and take note: *recognize* when it's time to ask for help, whether from a professional or a spiritual guide.

HAVE THE COURAGE TO SEEK HELP

I wasted so much time going to the gym and training the wrong way. I spent money, sacrificed an hour of my precious time every day, and battled procrastination—all for nothing. My efforts were in vain. The results I expected never came. Worse than that: I started to have back pain I'd never felt before.

One day I was at the gym doing exercises for my shoulders. An instructor approached me and asked, "How long have you been exercising that way?"

I smiled and replied, "For months!"

He shook his head and explained to me how that exercise was affecting my posture. That was the reason I had developed back pain!

On that day, I understood that all my training efforts would be in vain if I didn't get a *personal trainer*, someone who could teach me the right exercises step-by-step and show me the right way to use the equipment.

Many of us lack the courage to cry for help. We prefer to pretend everything is fine when we go to the gym. And although we don't have the slightest idea of what to do or how to use the equipment, we prefer to take the risk of injuring ourselves rather than seeking the right trainer who could help us obtain the results of our dreams.

In the two-in-one life, we need personal support—someone who can instruct us on *how* to do things. The best people to hold that role are therapists, pastors, and wise relatives. There is always someone around we may ask for help.

Choose carefully and wisely who you approach for help, as this person will have access to the intimate details of your life—but make the choice.

> **"There are people who rob us, others who give back to us."**
> **—Father Fábio de Melo**

GIVE YOURSELF TIME

Most people wish they had a "quiet life" in which everything was predictable. However, we need to understand that the progression of our life looks more like something we'd see on a heart-rate monitor than a ruler; the line of life is not straight but has high points and low points. Nevertheless, amid our ups and downs, we can be sure there's life.

When we're in one of the low points in life—when we're constantly arguing with our spouse, when we feel disconnected, when our marriage is struggling—it can seem like there's no end in sight to our hardship. At these times, it's vital to remember that time doesn't cure everything, but it can heal many hurts. Problems related to married life do not always get solved quickly. That's why patience is vital.

It can be difficult to know how to wait out a low point. However, many times, this is the only way to face a problem.

My wife and I have four children. Going to the hospital seems almost like a hobby! (That's not counting all the times we've taken the children to see their pediatrician.) We know that, when we arrive at the hospital, waiting in line is inevitable. I always bring a good book or have a podcast ready on my cell phone.

One day, I sat in the lobby of the emergency room reading a book for two hours while I waited for my son José to be seen. Suddenly Jeanine called me over and said, "It's time to go home!"

I had been concentrating on my book so hard, I looked up in surprise and asked, "What happened?"

Jeanine smiled and said, "We're done. José has his medicine. We're all set. Shall we go?"

On that day, the penny dropped: if waiting is the only way, find an "analgesic" to help you kill the time without experiencing pain.

> **If waiting is the only way, find an "analgesic" to help you kill the time without experiencing pain.**

Do you see what I'm saying?

The two-in-one marriage is the most intense relationship that exists, and it was designed to last until death. Fight to make your two-in-one marriage your favorite place to be.

Sometimes, it can feel as if giving up is the best thing you could do, but this is not true. Keep working at it. Fight for it. Great achievements are not reached easily but require sweat and energy. If you want to save your marriage, *show* it. If you want to say you love your spouse, *shout* it. Step up! Step up!

> **Fight to make your two-in-one marriage your favorite place to be.**

Q & A

Q: Tiago, I've followed you on social media for over two years. I understand the value of having a good relationship as a couple, but my husband is not as committed as I am. He seems to keep secrets, and he doesn't improve in basic things. It seems like any time now I'll receive devastating news or find out something overwhelming. I can't stand living under this tension. What is your advice?

A: Well, thank you for following me on social media. If you've been following me that long, you've certainly heard me speak about having your expectations aligned. Women and men get married for different reasons and expect opposite things. Before they get married, people rarely align with their soon-to-be spouse regarding their expectations for their future together. We simply fall in love, say we love each other, and go to the altar. In our heads, everything will be fine; love will keep us going. But divorce statistics reveal the number of bad choices we make as human beings, as well as the level of intolerance and lack of persistence.

I know a few ways of aligning a husband; today, I'll recommend just two. First, make sure he has an experience with God. I was born and raised in an evangelical church, and I've never seen a "crooked" man have an experience with God and keep on living the same way. I don't normally spiritualize things, but here there's no other way. There are things in a man that only the Holy Spirit is able to transform.

Second, encourage him to change his group of friends. The people we hang around with influence our expectations. When he starts to walk with men who love and honor their wives, with men who value their children, he will automatically be molded by the environment.

And, finally, don't give up. What God has joined together, let no one separate!

CONCLUSION

In this chapter, we learned some essential things about the most important interpersonal relationship—that of a husband and wife—with the two-in-one theory. In an ideal world, I would never need to approach this subject, since all matrimonial relationships would end only when one spouse dies, and this death would leave the widow or widower suffering, such was the love and partnership between them. In the real world, however, we see divorce plaguing more and more families everywhere.

In this chapter, I offered eight main points. They're so important, I'm going to list them out here so you can review them easily.

1.   Choose your life partner carefully.

2. Strive for coherency and prioritize your relationship.

3. Maintain the focus in your relationship so it remains healthy.

4. Work toward reciprocity.

5. Stay aligned in your expectations, ideologies, agenda, and lifestyle.

6. Beware of the enemies of marriage in the following areas: secrets, comparison, communication, discipline, physical intimacy, and money.

7. Surround your two-in-one relationship with people whom you aren't ashamed to approach for help.

8. Understand that time and patience are necessary for achieving the relationship you've dreamed of your whole life.

**In prosperity, our friends get to know us.
In adversity, we get to know our friends.**

5

JOY THIEVES

Some people spread happiness wherever they go;
others, whenever they go.
—Anonymous

In 2015, Disney Pixar released the movie *Inside Out*, and it's one of those kids' movies that offer great lessons for adults. If you haven't watched it, I highly recommend it! It follows eleven-year-old Riley as she moves to a different city with her parents and sees her life transformed. What's really interesting is that the main characters telling her story are her emotions: Joy, Sadness, Fear, Disgust, and Anger.

Memories, along with emotions, hold a central position in the movie's plot, defining who Riley is and how she interacts with the world. As the movie progresses, we see the delicate interplay between memories and the feelings they evoke. The story is riddled with humor and drama but is ultimately thought-provoking. Indeed, in an interview in the magazine *Veja Saúde*, neuropsychologist Cleide Lopes was asked what we can learn about our emotions from *Inside Out*. She responded this way: "All memories a person has, whether good or bad, bring feelings with them."[14]

I have found that it is typically the *people* who pass through our lives that most prominently take up residence in our memories. The paths of our lives are full of relationships with people. Some of them cross our paths and bring us sorrow. Others cross our paths and make us smile—or send chills down our spine.

Those descriptions probably brought a particular person to your mind, didn't they? What memories did they evoke? What feelings have arisen? Does thinking of the person associated with those descriptions make you sigh longingly? (Oh, how I miss them!) Or does it make you sigh in relief? (Good riddance!)

Throughout the course of our lives, we'll inevitably encounter people who steal our joy, who take captive our happiness. This wouldn't be so in the ideal world, of course. But, as I keep reminding you, unfortunately we're not living in the ideal world. In this real world, we live alongside a variety of toxic 1and complicated people. They are the envious, the vengeful, the prideful, the procrastinators, the lazy ones, the ones who hate you for the same reason others love you. Some people are a combination of these characteristics!

These kinds of people have existed since the beginning of the world. In the ancient book of the prophet Zechariah, we find necessary instruction on dealing with difficult people: *"Do not plot evil against each other"* (Zechariah 8:17). It's therefore not surprising that today we find ungrateful people, indifferent people, troublemakers, persecutors, liars, phonies, hypocrites, those who always play the victim, irresponsible people, people who never meet our expectations, influential thieves, and traitors like the renowned Judas. I could go on, but this list suffices to help us grasp the enormity of our daily struggle to keep healthy relationships with others.

Dealing with people is not an easy task. It's truly a challenge!

14. André Biernath, "9 Coisas Que O Filme *Divertida Mente* Ensina Sobre O Cérebro e As Emoções," *Veja Saúde*, February 14, 2016, https://saude.abril.com.br/bem-estar/9-coisas-que-o-filme-divertida-mente-nos-ensina-sobre-o-cerebro-e-as-emocoes/. Translation mine.

Dealing with people is not an easy task. It's truly a challenge! However, it's a challenge we all must rise up to, because we, as people, need people! Let's explore further what it looks like to deal with thieves of joy—and to emerge unscathed from our encounters with them.

THIEVES OF PEACE AND JOY

Rio de Janeiro was my home for thirty years. Having grown up in a suburb of this "Cidade Maravilhosa," or "Wonderful City," I unfortunately became accustomed to violence—particularly with robberies, which were seemingly routine in the region.

Once, when Jeanine was eight months pregnant with our first child, Julia, four robbers held me up in front of my parents' house. Besides taking all my things, they threatened to kill me. They stole my watch, my cell phone, all the money in my wallet, and my wedding ring. Since I was on the phone with Jeanine at the time, she heard everything and nearly fainted.

Today, living in Orlando, Florida, I realize how much that time in Rio contributed to making me street smart. I almost always recognize when someone approaching me has bad intentions. I've also come to recognize how much it damaged the quality of my mental life. In Rio, when I would see a motorcycle approaching, my heart would begin to race; I would break out in a cold sweat and begin to panic. This familiar panic sometimes still descends on me, vestiges of my multiple experiences of being robbed at gunpoint.

Even so, I firmly believe that car thieves and robbers do less damage than thieves of joy, captors of peace, and robbers of dreams. Even Jesus, in the Gospel of Matthew, calls us to put into perspective the value of physical belongings:

Do not store up for yourselves treasures on earth, where moths and vermin destroy, and where thieves break in and steal. But store up for yourselves treasures in heaven, where moths and vermin do not destroy, and where thieves do not break in and steal. For where your treasure is, there your heart will be also. (Matthew 6:19–21)

An expensive wristwatch? You can buy another one. But what about your peace? Thieves of peace can wreak havoc in your world. But what about thieves of joy? The damage they do in your life is perhaps more subtle, but these types of thieves are so common, their damage comes in quantity.

A close friend bought a beautiful pickup truck one day and was so happy with his purchase. He'd locked in a great interest rate on his loan and was thrilled by his truck's features. His smile could be seen a mile away.

As he parked at his neighborhood bakery to buy some fresh bread, a neighbor passing by sneered and called out his open window, "Nice car! It's a pity its color will make it so hard to sell later on."

One line—just one line—and the joy of that purchase was gone!

Joy thieves are more common than you think. They are everywhere: in your family, in your classes at school, in your church, in the grocery store, and in your workplace.

In this chapter, I want to teach you how to identify thieves of peace and joy and to shield yourself from them.

THE POWER OF CHOICE

Sigmund Freud, the father of psychoanalysis, said that the character of a man is formed by the people he chooses to live with. When it comes to the people in your life—with the exception of the unavoidable ones we discussed earlier—you get to choose who stays and who goes!

There are people who enter our lives by chance. However, they don't stay by chance. Some people should just pass through your life, while others should stay forever. The decision is yours. You choose the people who will forge your character. Use your own sense of purpose in life, your maturity, and your relationship with God to make this decision that will change your destiny.

UNAVOIDABLE JOY THIEVES

What about that next-door neighbor who is a joy thief, that relative who is an emotional captor, or that coworker who is a peace robber? These people are part of your spheres of friendship (chapter

1) or are unavoidable ones (chapter 2). How do you deal with them—people who you'd like to leave behind but simply can't? Sometimes it is possible, instead of blocking people for good, to minimize the time you spend with them. Perhaps you can change where you hang out, making sure it's somewhere they don't go (making them an avoidable one; see chapter 3). Other times, it's impossible to move away from these people. How difficult it is!

How do you choose who should depart from your life? This is my personal philosophy: when there is an apology, but not a word of forgiveness... when there is always an explanation, but never repentance...the best thing to do is to nip it in the bud.

> **When there is an apology, but not a word of forgiveness...when there is always an explanation, but never repentance...the best thing to do is to nip it in the bud.**

Do you know what this means? Never measure a person by her errors but by her ability to repent and fix things. People will always make mistakes, but just a few will go through the effort of repenting and trying to fix things. Value these precious few!

Consider these two disciples of Jesus. We discussed them briefly in chapter 1. Peter (Jesus's close friend) and Judas (Jesus's necessary friend) both screwed up in their relationship with Jesus. One denied Him, and the other betrayed Him. (See Luke 22.) Both wronged the Man to whom they'd sworn fidelity. The similarities end there. Peter repented and returned to Jesus's side to try to fix things; Judas, on the other hand, left and killed himself. (See Matthew 27:3–10.)

Believe me, people will help decide their own fate in your relationship. Some will do whatever they can to seek reconciliation. In these cases, be humble and seize the opportunity to repair the relationship. Others will simply turn their backs and disappear forever. In these cases, let them go.

A LESSON FROM WATER

Throughout this book, we've established that people are like stones: they're an inevitable part of our path, come in different forms, and must be dealt with in unique ways. The thieves of joy we're discussing in this chapter aren't the pebbles you pluck out of your shoe or the concrete blocks you put to use in building your success. No, these people are rocks smack-dab in the middle of your path, embedded into the dirt, ready to make you trip and stumble. How do we deal with these people?

When a spiritually cold person who is out of touch with their emotions encounters a rock in their path, their instinct is to kick it out of the way. Yet such people hurt only themselves; the rock won't move, and it doesn't feel anything when it is struck—but the person who kicked it hobbles away with an aching toe.

Kicking away the rocks on your path is not the best way to deal with them. If you kick them, you will be the one to get hurt—you and only you! So how *should* we act when we encounter them?

We can take a lesson from a stream of water. When you watch a stream running through a field, you'll notice that, although the water encounters many rocks in its path, it does not stop to confront or interact with each one; instead, it elegantly and quickly skirts around them, one by one. Running water will always follow its path, regardless of the number of rocks in its way.

If only we behaved like water! Instead of wasting time combating the rocks in our lives, we would just move forward around them. Dealing with rocks is as simple as this: master your emotions and avoid kicking the rocks in your path. If you do so, you'll go a long way in protecting yourself from the pain of the impact.

Master your emotions and avoid kicking the rocks in your path. If you do so, you'll go a long way in protecting yourself from the pain of the impact.

PICKING UP THE HINTS

People are unpredictable, but they reveal who they are in how they act and how they react. And everybody offers us hints of who they really are, even when they play a role to try to relate to you. Judas betrayed Jesus for thirty silver coins, but before he did that, he showed signs that there was something wrong his relationship toward money. The Bible says he would steal from the offerings and alms Jesus's ministry received. (See John 12:5–6.)

The people who betrayed you left hints before they did it, but you didn't connect the dots. Being a people specialist requires that you pay attention and learn from your experiences. You have to pay attention to the details of each person's behavior and to the words they speak.

For instance, when someone speaks ill of others to you, it's a sign that one day this person will speak ill of you to others. This is the cycle of relationships and coexistence. Socrates is quoted as saying, "Strong minds discuss ideas, average minds discuss events, weak minds discuss people."

Do you want to be surrounded by strong-minded people or weak-minded people? Identify which category someone belongs to, and then choose to draw closer or stay away from them. Select the people you want to keep around.

TYPES OF JOY THIEVES

Thieves of joy come in all shapes and sizes, but we can sort them into a few categories. Learning to identify thieves of joy will help you protect yourself against them. Let's look at what these thieves of joy can look like.

THE UNINTENTIONAL JOY THIEF

The unintentional joy thief makes negative comments about you or compares themselves with you, pointing out things they have that you don't, or achievements they've made that you haven't. Typically, the unintentional joy thief doesn't realize they're off base. They're not really interested in hurting you. They're not acting intentionally.

An unintentional joy thief might be the friend who arrives at your annual New Year's Eve party—the one you've spent weeks planning and preparing for—looks you over from top to bottom, and comments, "My coworker wore a dress just like yours last week." Nothing in the world will change because this friend's coworker wore a dress like yours. If she hadn't mentioned it, you wouldn't even have known it. But you can't stop thinking about her comment and feeling annoyed. Now, this friend has no idea that her mentioning this coincidence could annoy you or hurt you, so she sees no problem in making this comment during a night when you're already feeling a bit stressed. She unintentionally steals your joy.

There are many people like this—including, at times, each one of us.

UNINTENTIONALLY OFFENDING

There are some people who deserve your honest criticism, even if it's not pleasant to hear. For instance, if this person belongs to one of the three spheres of friendship we discussed in chapter 1, or if they're someone you mentor, it is worth mentioning how you might do something differently or make a different purchase. When you offer your feedback sensitively to people who trust you, you're adding something to their lives. Friends do that for each other! Perhaps keep your comments about your friend's ugly shirt to yourself until after that important work conference is over, though. Good friends also choose their timing carefully.

But if you're offering difficult feedback to someone who is not your friend, they're less likely to recognize that you are trying to help. Here's my advice in such cases: avoid stealing their joy! Instead, find a way to focus on the positive.

There's a movie in which the main character was the guy everybody liked. His secret? He would never steal anybody's joy. In one scene, a rather unattractive woman greeted him. He looked her in the eye, smiled, and said, "Your cheekbones are amazing. They are the perfect shape and turn pink when you get embarrassed." His sincere praise made that woman's day—maybe even her week.

I always pay special attention to what I say when someone shows me their work or talks about their achievement. Sometimes I don't even like what they share, but I'm not going to tell them that. I make a conscious decision not to steal their joy.

"But, Tiago, is it ever safe to speak honestly?" you might ask.

Of course it is. You can always find something to sincerely praise. If your friend's dress isn't to your taste, praise her beautiful smile, her hair, her jewelry, or her shoes instead. If you don't like the theme of someone's book, praise its cohesion. If you dislike the model of car your brother bought, praise its finish. You see? You can always find something to sincerely praise.

It's easy to accidently become an unintentional joy thief; it's easier still to train ourselves not to. Don't spoil somebody's moment. Don't be an unintentional joy thief!

STEALING JOY BY ELICITING ENVY

When my daughter Jasmim was born, my wife convinced me we needed a second car. The minivan I used to take our four kids, my mother-in-law, and our nanny all over town was no help if Jeanine and I needed to be in different places at the same time.

So, we went to an auto dealership. We were immediately struck by the number of shiny new cars on display. The salesman showed me four kinds of cars I could afford. To my surprise, a brand-new Mercedes-Benz was on the list. I got excited. Sure, the other cars he showed me offered the same comfort, but they didn't have that luxurious dash display, that caramel seat, that imposing Mercedes symbol. They weren't Mercedes-Benzes, after all.

My heart was inclined to the Mercedes-Benz because of the status and comfort it offered and the impression it made. In the rush of excitement, however, I tried to regain focus. I thought of people's reactions to my purchase. I knew that some people would love to see me in that car—but others would be enraged by it. I imagined myself arriving at a party in the Mercedes. The people in attendance would know me and be aware of who I am and what I do. I imagined those who couldn't afford a car like that would be thinking, "Well, he's apparently got money. He must be involved in something shady." Others would stay quiet but would start to envy my acquisition. I was sure other negative comments would run like water in a river. Even those who could buy a car nicer than mine might feel threatened. They might ask each other, "How can Tiago afford a car like that?

Has he closed a new deal? But he's a pastor too, isn't he? He must have used church funds for it."

That was when the penny dropped. Buying this car might make me a joy thief; it might steal others' joy—and it would certainly put me in the spotlight. I didn't want to do either of those things. I chose to buy the car that wasn't so flashy because I didn't want to make more enemies or spoil the joy of anyone less fortunate. (I have enough problems without provoking anyone. Imagine if I started looking for trouble!) Ultimately, the price of the car I bought was the same as that of the Mercedes, but the emotional impact it would have on people was different. In the end, my family was satisfied with the car, and I avoided offending my friends and "hidden enemies" (those who say they are friends but who in fact desire misfortune for me).

> **Before you share about a major achievement or significant purchase, form a mental picture of people's probable reactions; this will help you make the wise choice.**

In the ideal world, all people would celebrate each other's achievements and be gladdened by each other's victories. But we must remember that we're living in the real world, and in the real world, people envy each other, speak ill of others, and make excuses for why other people are able to achieve something they did not.

Now, I hope you don't walk away from this feeling like you can't by the things you really want. It's natural to express your joy after you buy that new computer or TV. Just be careful when you make purchases that you don't become an indifferent happiness thief in doing so. Be aware that there may be people who suffer when they see what you have. If you decide to squander your wealth, you're only increasing the gap between yourself and such people. Before you share about a major achievement or significant purchase, form a mental picture of people's probable reactions; this will help you make the wise choice.

GOSSIPING AND BEING CARELESS

Unintentional joy thieves certainly come in many forms. Some affect us over time, others in just a moment. For instance, there are people who hijack your emotions for a few hours by the things they post on social media or tell you in confidence. I know that I've been guilty of this. These people aren't necessarily trying to hurt you or get a reaction. Often they aren't even aware they're affecting you; this has certainly been true of me when I've shared content that has offended people.

Another type of unintentional joy thief is the gossiper—someone who shares things you've told them in confidence not because they want to harm you or expose you, but because they simply don't know how to control their tongues.

Bearers of bad news are another kind of unintentional joy thief. These people probably don't want to make you depressed, but because they are negative by nature, they are only capable of talking about tragedies and the like.

THE INTENTIONAL JOY THIEF

The intentional joy thief has varied reasons for appearing in your life. He's uncomfortable because you're happy in your marriage. She's annoyed that your boss likes you. He's envious that your neighbors celebrate when you're around. Ultimately, these joy thieves' justification doesn't matter; their motive is the same: to steal a little of your joy whenever they can.

The intentional joy thief doesn't act like this all the time with everyone, nor has he always behaved like this with you; rather, this person developed ill feelings toward you and now feels the need to strike you somehow.

Let me share an unpleasant example from my life. In the case I'm about to share, I myself was the intentional joy thief.

WEAPONIZING OUR SUCCESS

When I started my company at age twenty-five, I didn't have any resources. I was emotionally frustrated and would compare myself with everything and everyone. Jeanine explains well who I was at that time in the preface to my book *Dinheiro é Emocional* (*Money Is Emotional*).[15] You can check out that book for a perfect description of who I was.

When the company began to turn a profit, my credit score began to improve and I bought a brand-new car. My intention at that point was not to have more comfort or a reliable means of transport. No, I wanted to show everyone who had doubted me that, at that moment, I was fine. I also wanted to compete with my cousins and friends who had prospered before I did. I would insist on arriving late to family events or work appointments and parking my car right in front of the event location so everyone could see me arrive and recognize my success.

There was one particular friend to whom I always made sure to show off my newest acquisition. No matter what it was—a car, a watch, a cell phone—I was only satisfied after that friend saw it or admired my most recent achievement. I needed his affirmation.

Looking back, I can recognize how terribly I was conducting myself. How narrow-minded and ridiculous I was being! But at that time, I was completely blind—I just wanted to steal people's joy. I was enslaved by my frustrations and unattended desires.

People are like that! When they feel bad about themselves—when they view themselves as small and insignificant—they often try to be make themselves "bigger" by showing off the things they own. If you're desperate enough that you'll do anything, you will certainly choose to do the wrong thing! Have you ever felt this way, like you are willing to do anything to have others accept you?

> If you're desperate enough that you'll do anything, you will certainly choose to do the wrong thing!

RECOGNIZING THE ROOT PROBLEM

I've shared this miserable personal account with you to help you understand that *anyone can be an intentional joy thief.* A penchant for destruction is

---

15. Tiago Brunet, *Dinheiro é Emocional: Saúde emocional para ter paz financeira* (São Paulo: Editora Vida, 2018).

not a prerequisite. Ordinary people who don't watch out and take care of their feelings may turn into joy thieves. Back then, the problem wasn't my relatives or my friends; it was that my emotions were totally out of control, and I suffered from a lack of identity and spiritual smallness.

Fortunately, the people who steal your joy today may not do so in the future. People change. *I* changed. Back then, ensuring others recognized my success felt like a kind of emotional protection, a way to feel better about myself and more accepted. Today, it is the least of my concerns.

Because I've suffered my own stint as a joy thief, I'm able to be more empathetic toward the joy thieves I encounter. I can understand why some people are determined to hurt us and steal our joy. It's not that they have anything against us—it's that they need to make themselves feel better somehow, and they do that by making others feel worse. Having recognized this error in myself and corrected it, I'm able to withhold judgement and have a greater facility to forgive those who intentionally try to steal my joy.

We've all been victims of intentional joy thieves—but have you ever stolen someone else's joy?

Perform a self-analysis. Identify all your mistakes and be very critical of yourself. This will help you to understand others better.

FORGIVENESS PRESERVES FRIENDSHIP

The 2004 comedic film *Envy* tells the story of two close friends and neighbors, Tim and Nick. Nick invites Tim to be his partner in the research and release of an unusual product: a pet feces vaporizer. Tim doesn't give much credit to the idea and declines Nick's invitation.

When the product is a great success, making Nick very rich indeed, Tim is overcome by envy. He has to endure his wife and children asking him why they don't have all the things Nick has. Then, Tim accidently kills Nick's horse—and a good part of the plot is devoted to him trying to hide his mistake.

People are like this: instead of apologizing, they try to hide their mistakes!

Nick decides to give half of his company to Tim. Finally, Tim comes clean and tells Nick about the horse. Nick promptly forgives him, saying, "Really, it was an accident."

In the end, the vaporizer is withdrawn from the market and both guys lose everything. But when Tim approaches Nick with his own great idea—an innovative Pocket Flan—Nicks gets on board immediately and they become partners again.

People are like this: best friends make mistakes, but forgiveness corrects them!

THE NEUROTIC[16]

When a person feels that they are being persecuted, their anguish and anxiety are agitated. Believing you are a victim of persecution changes the way you approach the world—and it can cause you to become a joy thief. Neurotic joy thieves believe the world is against them and that everyone on earth is competing against them. In response, they try to hurt others emotionally and to spoil other people's joy.

Sometimes the neurotic joy thief chooses a specific victim to attack. More often, he opens fire and shoots his emotional upheavals and spiritual tragedies on anyone who crosses his path.

I lived with a neurotic joy thief some time ago. Early on, he and I were friends. He seemed to be a well-adjusted person with a good heart. He was doing much better than I was, both financially and professionally, so I saw him as someone to look up to. This is fairly typical of neurotic joy thieves; they have an incredible ability to disguise themselves.

Since I was both emotionally and financially broke when we met, he felt comfortable with me. After all, compared to me, he was "the man." Looking back, I can see that he was an unintentional joy thief. Even though he was aware I was going through hard times, he insisted on showing off the sports cars he bought or the watch that cost him who knows how much. I don't believe he was doing this to offend me. As I said, I wasn't a threat to him at that time.

16. Neurosis, or neuroticism, is a psychological disorder that leads the patient to suffer intense anguish and anxiety and to experience constant worry. I use the term "neurotic" only as an identifier of the type of joy thief I'm describing and not in its medical sense.

Time passed, and I grew closer to fulfilling my destiny. Every day I was preparing myself a little more, strengthening my faith, and balancing my emotions. Over time, small results began to emerge, like a flower blooming in the desert—small and fragile, but nevertheless beautifully conspicuous in those acres of lifeless landscape. I was leaving behind my financial lukewarmness and ministerial and professional paralysis.

When things started to change for the better in my life, this "friend" called me and said, "Tiago, why are you bad-mouthing me out there?"

"What are you talking about? I haven't said anything bad about you," I replied. "We're friends! Let's figure this out. If you want to talk to me face-to-face, we can do that today."

He never tried to resolve our friendship, although I always proposed quick fixes.

As time went by, he got worse. The better my life got, the more he would plot to steal my peace. He would make up terrible stories about me and tell them to others, trying to compromise my reputation.

I probably could have taken him to court for the lies he was telling about me, but I decided to go another route. I simply walked away from what I'd thought was our friendship.

One day, when I was trying to pick up the emotional pieces of my life, I was invited to give a lecture for which I would receive compensation. I was just beginning my career in public speaking. Everything was new and exciting to me. Just hours before the event, this former friend called me to say, "I know you're about to participate in this event, but I think you should know that so-and-so is going to sue you for all you're worth."

The ground fell out from beneath me. My mind went unfocused. Why did he have to deliver this news to me right then? Couldn't it have waited?

DEVELOPING EMPATHY

The neurotic happiness thief doesn't care about bringing you bad news on the best day of your life. He's a killjoy by nature. It's really hard to understand or love someone like this. However, if you want to be an expert on people, you need to understand why people do what they do. That's what calms me down: understanding the *why* of things!

Every abuser—whether sexual or emotional—was abused by somebody. The same is true of the neurotic joy thief: he was hurt by somebody. Perhaps he was abandoned by his father when he was still in his mother's womb. Perhaps that warrior woman, who was left with the challenge of raising her kids without a father, had no other option at that time but to prostitute herself. Poverty, mistreatment, and shame were part of her daily routine.

I know that my persecutor endured a childhood that I would never have been able to bear. He survived, but when he grew up and saw the people around him starting to surpass him, he didn't have the emotional intelligence or flexibility to cope. He went on the attack.

When I understood this, my anger left me, and a feeling of compassion filled me instead.

Understanding the *why* is an important tool for constructing your emotional health. Even if the other party is the wrongdoer, if you don't solve your inner problems, you'll be the one who is psychologically damaged!

ADMIRABLE FROM AFAR

Look around you. It may seem that your coworker's wife is perfect, that your neighbor's son is nice, that your competitor's employees are the best. But, in the words of Millôr Fernandes, "How admirable are those we don't know well!"

That's just life, and people are like this. You live with them for a while and the fascination is over.

In the ideal world, all people would be excellent in what they do and would contribute collectively. In the real world, though, people are selfish, and the closer we get to people, the less we care for them and the less we admire them. It's no wonder that the unavoidable ones are those closest to us! (See chapter 2.)

That's why I try not to get impressed with those whom I don't know yet. When we reach a certain level of intimacy, everything changes. The opposite can also be true! Believe me: there are people I know today who are easier to admire when you get to know them than just after you've met them.

People specialists are those who know how to deal with other people to the point that those around them admire them. They are the ones who understand that the substance is worth much more than the appearance.

MOVING TARGETS

Who is more likely to be assaulted when they are walking down the street in a major city: the guy wearing a golden watch and a chain around his neck, or the guy wearing shorts and a T-shirt?

Whether we mean to or not, we wear things, write things, and share things that awaken the beast. The popular saying "Opportunity makes the thief" speaks true in this context. The Bible also issues this warning: *"Be alert and of sober mind. Your enemy...prowls around like a roaring lion looking for someone to devour"* (1 Peter 5:8).

As people specialists, we shouldn't make ourselves prone to emotional assaults. Believe me, there's no use in provoking joy thieves because you want to show off or erase some past frustration by showing others what you have now.

Joy thieves are cruel and know your weaknesses. They live on sadness, and you are searching for happiness.

Folks, this is really serious!

One time I was standing in a room full of important people when I heard one particularly influential guy mention the name of a strategic friend of mine. It caught my attention immediately, and I paid close attention to what he and his companions were saying.

The first man said, "And what about so-and-so"—referring to my friend—"isn't he a philanthropist and very religious? I can't understand it! He posted a photo wearing a Louis Vuitton belt and showing off a car with red seats. I bet it was a Maserati."

The conversation was getting serious now, and one of his companions said, "That's why he's no longer welcome in my town."

The first man grabbed the hook and continued, "Do you want to live in the rain, brother? You're gonna get wet! I'd like to see his income tax records to see if he can afford everything he's showing off."

The man they were talking about is a good friend of mine, a family man, and a very nice person. Do you know what his sole mistake was? He had posted a photo of himself inside a car wearing a belt with a visible brand name. This was enough to provoke, although unintentionally, some joy thieves.

I went through something similar, but, in my case, I was the joy thief.

A friend of mine released a book and then posted a video on social media, joyfully announcing he had won an important award from his publisher. As a writer, I am aware of all the awards that are given. When I saw his post, I started to criticize him in my mind. "What a lie!" I thought. "Awards are given by trade magazines, not publishers." As if this weren't bad enough, my inward tension kept building. "The guy just released the book and he's already bragging about it." And it got even worse: his announcement bothered me so much that I hit "unfollow" on his Instagram account.

No one is immune to toxic emotional attacks. Only then did I remember that being a people specialist doesn't mean being perfect or never feeling negative things. After all, no one is immune to toxic emotional attacks. But being a people specialist does require me to identify what is happening internally and then quickly open my toolbox to fix the problem.

I started to reflect on what I was feeling and wondered if my negative feelings were something real or the result of some loose bolts in my emotions.

I consider myself a balanced person, but nobody is immune to provocation. In this case, the way the post was worded, its topic (which I could relate to), and my personal circumstances at the moment I read it led me to react negatively. After a couple minutes, however, I opened my toolbox and got to work internally by asking myself these key questions:

+ Who am I?

+ Do I need to feel this to prove who I am?

+ Why did I get so upset?

+ Am I jealous, or is he really exaggerating?

+ What can I do today to ensure I don't feel this way again tomorrow?

+ Does my happiness depend on my attitude or another person's post?

That person, so special and talented, was provoking me without even knowing it; if I hadn't used my emotional toolbox, he could have lost my friendship or even gained an enemy. If I, who consider myself emotionally healthy, was about to block my friend and even speak ill of him, how often must those people who make up almost 80 percent of the population who struggle emotionally react in a similarly negative way, or worse?[17]

PROTECTIVE TOOLS

Do we have any hope of shielding ourselves against joy thieves? People specialists need to grow daily in order to protect themselves from joy thieves. Over the next few paragraphs, I'll present to you a set of protective tools.

KNOW YOURSELF

My name is Tiago da Costa Brunet. I was born in Corumbá, Mato Grosso do Sul, because my father, still a typical Rio de Janeiro citizen, was serving in the Brazilian Navy in Corumbá's neighboring city of Ladário.

Today, at age thirty-eight, I help millions of people through videos available online, live events, and books. I'm a constant defender of social and educational causes in Brazil and Africa.

I'm married to Jeanine, whom I love and who has always taken care of me and our four children. We are parents to Julia, José, Joaquim, and Jasmim. And this is, to me, the most important title I bear: father. This makes me whole. My dreams have all come true in my family.

---

17. A study conducted primarily by Jonathan Schaefer revealed that although the percentage diagnosed is lower, the real number of people in need of emotional care is about 80 percent of the world's population. See Aaron Reuben and Jonathan Schaefer, "Mental Illness Is Far More Common Than We Knew," *Scientific American*, July 14, 2017, https://blogs.scientificamerican.com/observations/mental-illness-is-far-more-common-than-we-knew/.

I am the son of Dario, a pastor who had a calling but who also worked in the military, and Fani, an elementary school teacher who left her job to raise her kids. These two are my best friends to this day.

I have two wonderful brothers who are talented and gifted. From time to time, we argue in the best "street fight" style, but, afterward, everything is fine.

I'm a pastor, educator, international speaker, writer, and teacher of online courses. My fruit can be seen in my family; in the number of people converted monthly to the gospel of Jesus, which I preach; in my social networks; in my financial life; and in my faithful and constant friends, whom I have kept since my childhood.

This is Tiago. This is me. I know who I am.

Do you know why I'm telling you all this? Because every day we're challenged to forget who we are when we are provoked or find ourselves in a difficult situation. Knowing and remembering who you are in difficult times will help you make wise decisions and remain true to yourself.

Let me give you an example. Long ago, I had to travel with all my family from Brazil back home to the United States. We had spent our vacation with our children's grandparents in Rio de Janeiro. It was a very special time for them.

On the plane, my third son, Joaquim, began to cry nonstop. He was certainly making a scene. I took him in my arms and carried him to the corridor between economy and first class where there was a small kitchen and a bathroom. I spent a few minutes there with him, grateful to have found a good spot to distract my little one.

A religious leader came out of the first-class cabin to use the toilet and saw me standing there. He smiled and, without greeting me, asked, "Are you in an economy seat? I haven't seen you in first class."

I don't know if he meant any harm, but I felt as if I had been attacked. Rather than allowing this feeling to overcome me and take over, I protected my heart and replied, "My family and I are back there in economy. We'll survive." He smiled and left.

I returned to my seat. Hours later, I was already stressed because Joaquim still wouldn't stop crying and yelling. Finally, the plane landed, and we disembarked and made our way to the long immigration line. The religious leader and his wife were right ahead of us. She looked me over from top to bottom and then turned away.

You're probably wondering why this couple was making me feel so riled up. Well, there's something I haven't told you yet: my wife and I knew them. We had dined with them several times. I had previously lectured at the institution this man presides over. And he and his wife were treating me like a stranger!

I wondered why they were showing me all that contempt, but before I could give birth to an emotional ghost, I remembered who I am.

Identity!

"I'm Tiago. I help people, I don't do harm to anyone. I'm a father of four incredible kids; I'm here with the person I love the most—my wife. Whatever is going on, it doesn't have to do with me. They are the ones who are probably not doing okay."

Right there in line, I prayed, "Lord, teach me the fear of Your name. Make me a humble servant of all. Thank You, Holy Spirit!"

Just by reminding myself of who I am and praying, I protected my heart from a conflict that could have dragged on for years.

NEVER REACT IN THE MOMENT

What the Bible calls *temperance*, emotional intelligence and science would call *self-control*. This is the most useful tool to use when you're facing a problem.

It can be difficult to practice self-control when the attack comes from an unavoidable one because there is an emotional burden involved. When someone you've never seen before swears at you in traffic, it has an emotional impact; when your coworker swears at you, it creates a tsunami. In both situations, reacting is *never* an option.

I challenge you to find any example from history where someone made the right choice by reacting aggressively when offended. Instead, Jesus exhorts us, *"Bless those who curse you, pray for those who mistreat you. If someone slaps you on one cheek, turn to them the other also. If someone takes your coat, do not withhold your shirt from them"* (Luke 6:28–29). That's what Jesus taught us: turn the other cheek to the aggressor. I'll give myself permission to add my own teaching here: pray for those who are making up stories about you. It seems silly, but, in truth, it's a war strategy. When you speak well of someone who is saying bad things about you, or when you turn the other cheek, you're shouting for everyone to hear: "I'm not going to react!"

When I was little, whenever I complained about troubles with my brothers, my mom would affectionately remind me, "When one does not want, three do not argue." If you react when provoked, you lose the battle. Whoever strikes expects retaliation. Without retaliation there is no war.

SKIP THE AVOIDABLE ONES, SUPPORT THE UNAVOIDABLE ONES

Wisdom is an amazing tool. It measures what we say and prompts us to think before we speak. Wisdom is all you need to jump in and support people. With wisdom, you learn to skip over joy thieves who are just stones in your way; and with wisdom, you are able to support the unavoidable ones in your life.

How are you to live surrounded by unavoidable joy thieves? Here are some precious tips:

+ Understand that this person is emotionally ill and therefore does not want to reach a point of peace.

+ Promote a peaceful environment. As long as it's in your control, avoid going on the offense.

+ Focus not on the joy thief but on the divine plan that decided this person should be in your life in whatever role they hold (e.g., relative, coworker, etc.). Remember that God has already seen your future and knows that you will need to go through this process somehow.

TREAD CAREFULLY ON SOCIAL MEDIA

Recently, I was giving a lecture to two thousand entrepreneurs and said this: "Don't believe what you see on social media. Even I have never posted something that was 100 percent real."

Everyone was shocked. I continued, "Folks, I've never posted any of the arguments I've had with Jeanine; I only post photos where we're smiling or in a beautiful place. I've never posted photos of when I've hitchhiked somewhere in an old car; I only post when some businessman sends a jet or a helicopter to pick me up, and I make it sound like that's my normal day-to-day. I shrink my belly, use filters, and post forced smiles."

And I didn't stop there! I continued, "This is what social media is. It was created for appearances, not for reality. Why do we still use social media as a standard for comparison? Nobody posts a late payment notice; they post a picture of the car in the garage. Nobody posts the twenty-four installments they need to pay to cover their trip; they post the photos they took at the Eiffel Tower."

If something hurts you, stop looking at it. Stop following that person. Just forget it. Be selective about the kind of people you follow on social media, the topics you search for, and the amount of time you dedicate to it.

EVOLVE SPIRITUALLY

This final tool I'll offer you is really important: grow in your spiritual life.

The ability to practice gratitude, to serve those who will never be able to give you anything in return, to love those who don't even like you—all of these are spiritual attributes.

Evolving as a spiritual being has nothing to do with going to church or listening to sermons. The spiritual development I'm talking about looks more like magnifying the attributes that only those who have decided to strengthen the spirit and weaken the flesh can understand.

In particular, I suggest you learn more about Christianity. It was born as a religion based on the teachings of Jesus Christ, and it permeates all aspects of our life. Jesus taught the crucial points for a healthy spiritual life: loving, forgiving, repenting, and serving.

Whoever is interested in what the Bible refers to as "works of the flesh"— namely, prostitution, greed, revelry, drunkenness, enmity, and so on—may never understand the importance of being grateful, of serving the lowest members of society, and of loving those who persecute them.

Think about it: joy thieves are out there, but there are people who have spent their entire lives in communities filled with vulnerabilities and have never been afflicted.

Take the time to foster your spiritual maturity. If you do, you'll find you are much stronger and more resilient the next time you encounter a joy thief.

JESUS: THE GOOD SAMARITAN

Jesus was a great storyteller. To reach the hearts of His followers, Jesus used parables—highly relatable fictitious stories that applied to the lives of His listeners. One of Jesus's most famous parables is the parable of the good Samaritan. In addition to offering a poignant message on how to treat others, the account in which we find the parable, Luke 10:25–37, offers us an excellent example of how to interact with someone bent on stealing our joy.

This passage opens with a teacher of the Jewish law, full of pride, sarcasm, and irony, challenging Jesus with a question. *"On one occasion an expert in the law stood up to test Jesus. 'Teacher,' he asked, 'what must I do to inherit eternal life?'"* (Luke 10:25). Notice that this so-called expert approaches the Master with the intention of contradicting, embarrassing, and discrediting Him; at the very least, he hopes to provoke a response from Him. Notice moreover that when he addresses the Messiah, he calls Him *"Teacher,"* or, in some translations, *"Master."* This address drips with irony, of course. How could someone who wanted to hurt his target address him sincerely as *"Teacher"*?

What that man probably didn't know was that Jesus was emotionally shielded. The One he sought to provoke carried the fruit of the Spirit, including the characteristics of gentleness and self-control.

The Messiah never allowed Himself to be carried away by irony or brought down by other people's arrogance. But we allow it frequently, don't we? We pick fights, refuse to take an insult, express everything we feel, and live out the infamous "eye for an eye." Following Jesus's example, we must decide whether we want to be right or whether we want to influence people in a positive way. Jesus changed the world with His influence without ever fighting to be right.

Jesus answers His emotional tormentor's questions like any wise person should: by asking questions. He asks this expert of the Jewish law, *"What is written in the Law?...How do you read it?"* (Luke 10:26). By asking "What is written?" Jesus takes the responsibility of answering off His own shoulders. By asking "How do you read it?" the Messiah again places the responsibility back on His questioner. Jesus was very intelligent! The malicious law expert must have felt annoyed. He probably thought, "What wisdom is this that reverses the position of the attack? I came to argue, but now I'm the one being confronted!"

If we had Jesus's emotional intelligence, would anything be impossible?

The Jewish expert answers Jesus's questions by offering the following summary of the law: *"'Love the Lord your God with all your heart and with all your soul and with all your strength and with all your mind'; and, 'Love your neighbor as yourself'"* (Luke 10:27). Jesus approves of the man's answer—but the man isn't done asking questions. Luke records that the man *"wanted to justify himself, so he asked Jesus, 'And who is my neighbor?'"* (Luke 10:29).

Has anyone ever done this to you—tried to trap you with their questions? Have you noticed there are always people who think they are better than everyone else and look for ways to ask questions and provoke situations that will wound others? Jesus was an expert on dodging these kinds of people.

Notice how Jesus handles this man. He *doesn't beat the irony, but neither is He indifferent to the Jewish expert's malicious approach.* The Gospels show us that many people tried to knock down Jesus with emotional attacks, asking Him malicious questions, spreading absurd gossip, calling Him horrible names, and casting doubt on His true identity. Do you know why they attacked His emotions rather than attacking Him legally or financially? Because the greatest war that people face is fought on the battlefield of emotions! He who wins in emotions wins all the rest. Do you understand?

> *Above all else, guard your heart, for everything you do flows from it.*
> (Proverbs 4:23)

From Jesus, we can learn to respond to emotional insults in the right way. Jesus didn't respond to insults the way most people would. He didn't attack anyone with accusations. Instead, He provoked them to think critically. When Jesus wanted to open someone's mind (knowing that people always have a closed mind until someone opens it), He would tell stories that related to the practical issues His audience faced on a daily basis. As a result, those who heard His parables would identify with one of the characters. But these weren't just any stories; the parables Jesus told contained the secrets of His kingdom.

From Jesus, we can learn to respond to emotional insults in the right way.

Jesus's answer is not only one of His greatest teachings, but it also shows us what a people specialist He is. Here is the parable He tells:

> *A man was going down from Jerusalem to Jericho, when he was attacked by robbers. They stripped him of his clothes, beat him and went away, leaving him half dead. A priest happened to be going down the same road, and when he saw the man, he passed by on the other side. So too, a Levite, when he came to the place and saw him, passed by on the other side. But a Samaritan, as he traveled, came where the man was; and when he saw him, he took pity on him. He went to him and bandaged his wounds, pouring on oil and wine. Then he put the man on his own donkey, brought him to an inn and took care of him. The next day he took out two denarii and gave them to the innkeeper. "Look after him," he said, "and when I return, I will reimburse you for any extra expense you may have."*
>
> (Luke 10:30–36)

Jesus tells a parable in which a man is beaten by a gang of robbers and left for dead on the side of the road. A Samaritan finds him and, unlike the others, who had passed him by without a second glance, he stops, tends to his wounds, and takes him to an inn. It's such a simple story, but it delivers an essential truth: some people hurt; others heal. Life goes on!

Joy thieves stole that man's health and prosperity, but a good man gave it all back. Life is like that. *People* are like that, as you've seen throughout this book!

With this parable, Jesus paints a scene worthy of a movie. The characters in this story are:

- The expert of the law: ironic, malicious, and envious, who seeks to bring down anyone who stands out

- Jesus: the people specialist

- The thieves: those who only steal what others have

- The beaten man: wounded, vulnerable, and in need of help

Which character do you relate with? What kind of person are you?

Jesus concludes His parable by asking the man another question: *"'Which of these three do you think was a neighbor to the man who fell into the hands of robbers?'" The expert in the law replied, 'The one who had mercy on him.' Jesus told him, 'Go and do likewise'"* (Luke 10:36–37).

Q & A

Q: Tiago, I completed the course "Be a People Specialist," and so much has changed in my life and in my relationships. A question that I still have concerns my mom: she is somewhere between an unintentional and a neurotic joy thief; she insists on giving me bad news that ruins my week, and she goes out of her way to make me unhappy. How should I react to this?

A: Well, we discussed your issue in this chapter. Unavoidable joy thieves make us suffer a lot, in part because they should instead be the reason for our joy.

Compassion, which is the evolution of empathy, is what we need in these cases. Parents, however bad they may seem, don't steal our joy with the intention of hurting for hurt's sake (with a few exceptions). In general, they think they are protecting their children, or they are simply transferring their frustrations and pain to you.

I also advise you to use the tool of spiritual growth: try to serve and love those who are closest to you, always forgiving them as quickly as possible. In addition, remember not to share with such people every detail of your life, only those necessary for coexistence; that way, there is less risk that your joy will be stolen.

CONCLUSION

In the ideal world, all people would live happily and have gratitude for all their possessions and achievements. However, in the real world, this often doesn't happen, and many people take pleasure in killing your joy and making your day difficult. They are like true rocks on the road.

In this chapter, you learned how to deal with joy thieves. You were reminded that we need to have an accurate perception of our reality. You learned what kinds of joy thieves you'll meet: the unintentional, the intentional, and the neurotic.

I reminded you that appearances can be deceptive and that we should be careful not to provoke happiness thieves. Then, I concluded by exploring the protective tools you can use to shield yourself against joy thieves: knowing yourself; refraining from reacting in the moment; skipping the avoidable ones and supporting the unavoidable ones; treading carefully on social media; and trying to evolve spiritually.

Some people will cling to their past because they are failing to deal with their future.

6

THE LIFE TRAIL

"Success is to be measured not so much by the position that one has reached in life as by the obstacles which he has overcome."
—Booker T. Washington

I remember the first time I walked the Via Dolorosa in Jerusalem. Franciscan archeologists estimate that the route Jesus took to His crucifixion was around six hundred meters long, or a little over one-third of a mile.[18] The path taken by pilgrims traveling in His steps starts close to the Lion Gate, one of the main entrances to the Old City, and finishes at the Church of the Holy Sepulchre, the location of Jesus's grave prior to His resurrection according to the Catholic Church. This route includes fourteen stops or stations, each of which tells a part of the Master's experience leading up to being crucified. Jewish guides claim that Jesus fell at the third and seventh stations; it was at the seventh station that He could no longer bear the weight of the cross and was helped by Simon of Cyrene. (See Luke 23:26.) Even Jesus, whom we Christians consider

---

18. See Odalberto Domingos Casonatto, "Qual a distância que Jesus, percorreu com a cruz até ser crucificado? ["How far did Jesus carry the cross before being crucified?"], aBiblia.org, November 4, 2014, https://www.abiblia.org/ver.php?id=7878.

to be the Son of God, needed a shoulder to lean on. Imagine how much we mere mortals need each other!

Jesus progressed down a path after He was condemned to die. We too proceed through life down our own path. Indeed, living life is like traveling down a poorly marked road. We start this journey before anybody even knows we exist—at the moment of conception! From the moment we began to exist, we've traveled down our own personal path. Only when we leave this earth will our race be over. Until that point, we will get along best with ourselves and others if we understand at which stage we and those around us are at in our life's journey.

Let's go!

MILE MARKERS

When you travel down a highway, there are stops along the way. If you're thirsty, need to go to the bathroom, or need to fill up on gas, you take a break at a gas station or rest stop. Likewise, there are various situations along the path of life that may cause us to stop, slow down, or speed up as we make our way toward our planned destination.

Through my experience as a life coach, pastor, and mentor to hundreds of people, I've realized that life is made of stages and processes. We will not be successful if we do not face these stages. You may insist that your life or your story is unique. However, every person will go through the six stages I present in this chapter.[19]

It is enlightening to learn what part of your life's trail you are at right now. Being certain of the stage you're in helps you as you deal with yourself and those around you. Remember: you only change what you can identify!

19. Journalist Airton Ortiz famously said, "We are the result of the books we read, the trips we make, and the people we love." The theory I present to you in this chapter is the sum of everything I've learned during my decades of walking on my own life's trail. That trail has included much reading on subjects including interpersonal relationships, childhood development, character formation, self-knowledge, human development, theology, psychology, the behavior of men vs. women, influence, persuasion, and so on. I also draw from the new places, cultures, environments, and people I've encountered, as well as my experience as a pastor, counselor, coach, and teacher of thousands. I want to make it clear that I developed the theory of the life trail, and it is based on all my experiences and research. It's impossible to distinguish one thing from another and identify any one foundational experience for each one of the phases I present.

Every day, my team and I receive cries for help from people that sound like this: "Tiago, I'm feeling totally blocked!" "I'm taking such small steps." "I can't make the move I need to make!" Most people who write to me say they feel stuck or weighed down, as if they are carrying a huge burden. Some of them can't identify that burden; others identify it with various problems people experience: they were fired from their jobs, or had a problem in their childhood, or were left by their spouse, and so on. Some people also say they have just been surviving for a long time but not really living.

It is vital to know what point of the path you are on so that you don't linger too long at any one stop. It is essential that you situate yourself, identify your present stage, and move forward if necessary.

Let's begin by asking ourselves these questions:

+ Am I still at the beginning of my life?

+ Am I halfway through it?

+ Is there still time to recalculate my route if necessary?

+ Do I have the strength and help I need to finish the race?

+ Do I know what is at the end of this road?

> ## The coward is the one who doesn't take new paths in life, or use his strengths to face the obstacles on this path.
> ## —Jewish Text

God's Word tells us that on the road to Damascus, Saul, the infamous persecutor of Christians, had an encounter with the risen Jesus and was transformed into Paul the apostle (see Acts 9); it was then that he embarked on the next phase of his life. Before this encounter, he persecuted Christians; afterward, he became one of the most prominent gospel preachers of all time.

The path of life offers us experiences that align our purpose with our destiny. To become a people specialist, you will have to learn much more about yourself. Let's get started!

PHASE ONE: LEARNING AND ROLE MODELS

It is in this phase that both your concept and interpretation of people are born. Your way of seeing relationships arises in this period. Childhood shapes us, believe me! And this is true for you and for everyone you live with. Always remember this.

This is the first phase of life for anyone, whether rich, poor, Christian, Muslim, Jewish, overweight, slim, Japanese, white, or black. Phase one of your life trail is learning and modeling.

"Tiago, what does that mean? I don't get it," you might be saying.

Allow me to explain. In the first years of your life, you learn things that will determine how you will navigate this earthly life, and you will have both positive and negative role models.

Learning, like role models, can be a blessing or a curse.

Let's look at some examples. You may have had an uncle as a role model when you were little. But he was "smart," and that ended up becoming a negative reference to you. Perhaps your role model was a father who provided for your family but was prone to violence and would hit your mother. Or maybe your role model was your cousin who was always joyful and fun but who liked to talk negatively about people behind their backs. Thus, we have both good and bad role models; we learn both the good and positive and the bad and negative.

It's really important to remember that the things you say and the people you choose to hang around are shaped by the knowledge and behaviors you picked up in the first years of life.

> One thing is certain: you've been influenced by role models and shaped by the knowledge you acquired early on. Another thing is guaranteed: the people who influenced you early on were not perfect!

One thing is certain: you've been influenced by role models and shaped by the knowledge you acquired early on. Another thing is guaranteed: the people who influenced you early on were not perfect! During the periods of your childhood and early adolescence, you learned things such as love and hatred, respect and rebellion, honor and revolt. All of these things were modeled to you by the people you lived with and around.

Understand that many people surrounding you today whom you find difficult and hard to deal with had rough childhoods, during which they learned the wrong things from poor role models. That's why, when we study a person's childhood, we often find that the difficult behavior they exhibit as an adult has a correlating episode in their childhood that marked them. (For instance, those who practice deviant sexual behavior, who are extremely withdrawn or "restless" in this area, may have been victims of sexual abuse, had intimate physical contact at a young age, or were exposed to pornography early on.)

I once helped a young man whose father was taking him to brothels when he was eight years old. If this wasn't bad enough, his father would also force him to prostitute himself, even as a child. It's hard for many of us to even fathom this experience—but to this young man, it became a point of reference.

He started to have problems in adulthood, including mistreating women. This behavior was not his choice; it was something he had learned subconsciously because of his childhood experiences. His father's actions had taught him that women were to be used.

Many of the people who are wronging you today are doing so not because they are evil but because what they learned and had modeled for them in their childhood and early adolescence transformed them into who they are today. That's why the Bible says, *"Do not judge, or you too will be judged"* (Matthew 7:1). We don't know all the details of other people's pasts, how their standards were built, or what behaviors were modeled to them. Even if we do know their stories, it is impossible to know the extent of their misery. Therefore, it is vital that we practice the ancient wisdom of Matthew 7:1: *"Do not judge, or you too will be judged."* Why? Because each and every person has had varying role models and learning patterns; each of us has gone through different experiences that have shaped us into who we are today.

There are people who spent their childhood without any financial worries and were able to eat whatever they wanted and regularly went on vacation; others had to start working at the age of eight so they could eat and help feed the rest of their family. The learning and modeled behavior that shaped those who started working at age eight is different from the learning and modeled behavior that shaped those who always had enough.

The adult of today, the *you* of today, is the result of phase one of the path of life: learning and role models. The person you are today was shaped by what was said to you in your childhood, the experiences you had, and the things you saw and heard. All these things shaped you and became positive or negative knowledge for you. This is the beginning of our lives.

People make decisions on the path of life based on the learning and modeled behavior they received as children. Do I stop or keep going? Do I marry Tom, Dick, or Harry? Do I spend or save? Do I enjoy this moment or postpone the pleasure? Your decisions regarding each of these and all other questions in life are influenced by the learning and modeled behavior you received.

Many people today are suffering emotionally, financially, or in some other area because they lacked proper modeling and teaching during their childhood. They are totally ignorant when it comes to destiny, decision-making, and choosing friends.

The first phase of life is learning and role models. You didn't have a choice regarding the role models you had; they may have been left to chance or chosen by God. Either way, you learned from them.

> **"Life is like a bicycle. To keep your balance you must keep moving."**
> **—Albert Einstein**

PHASE TWO: TRIAL AND ERROR

The phase that comes after learning and role models is trial and error. In phase two, which typically aligns with your adolescence and youth, your decisions start to depend more on yourself. Many of them are exclusively yours. You've started to live your life. It is you who will choose whether to go to college, what job to pursue, and which person you will marry.

The second phase of life's trail is closely related to the first one. Based on what you learned and what was modeled for you, you will try new things in different areas of your life: in your professional life, your love life, business, friendships, and so forth. You will try things without having the slightest idea whether they are what you really want.

Most people today don't know exactly what they want. You may talk to someone who is studying veterinarian medicine simply because they like animals, but they're not sure if they really want to be a veterinarian. There are people who, on their wedding day, can't answer "yes" or "no" when you ask if they are sure about what they're doing.

People are not sure what to do because phase two is a time of uncertainty. It coincides with the end of adolescence and the beginning of adulthood. It is in this phase that people will always try, because in life you cannot keep still. Mistakes and frustration are a natural result of these attempts.

In phase two, you will make wrong choices, and so will the people around you. This will generate frustration.

Perhaps you are broken, frustrated, and stuck in a rut; or perhaps you simply want something new. Perhaps you want to study a new subject or have a personal experience with God. This phase, with the decisions you are required to make after experiencing frustrations, will generate an encounter with your purpose.

> ## Your frustrations may lead you to make decisions that will generate an encounter with your purpose.

Remember, your life path was forged in your mother's womb, and you set off down it the moment you exited her body;[20] within the first seconds after birth, you entered the phase of learning and role models. You didn't choose what you learned or who your role models were, yet they shaped who you are, particularly in the adolescence phase. In phase two, trial and error, you try to get married, try to start a business, try to go to college. You go through many

---

20. Although I believe life begins at conception, it is in the moment of birth that a person is considered alive. Before, a person is in formation.

frustrations until the moment in life arrives, maybe when you are thirty, forty, or fifty, when you say, "I can't stand this suffering anymore! I can't keep trying and getting frustrated." This cycle of attempts and frustration leads you to invest more time in your relationship with God or in your studies, pushing you to find your purpose! And when you find it, you discover the fruit of phase two.

Listen to the voice of experience: I've been through all of this. I've had my share of bad role models and negative teachings that shaped me. And these experiences from my past have allowed me to share with you a little of what I learned from all I went through and overcame. There are many people who think that my entire life was good; on the contrary, many parts of it were quite traumatic!

When I was twenty-two I decided to be an entrepreneur. I didn't want to suffer the severe hardships I had suffered in the past, nor did I want to depend on anyone else. Due to the role models I had as a child and the unconscious learning that took place in my childhood and early adolescence, I told myself I wanted to be a businessman. I clung to this belief and set out to become one.

I initially had several results that I considered positive. However, frustration soon set in. Eventually, my company went broke, and I lost nearly everything. The only thing I didn't lose was my family, but I almost destroyed my marriage. I was broke financially and broken emotionally. It was terrible. But it was in that phase, when I reached rock bottom, that I found my purpose and entered into the next phase of life. In my case, I found that my purpose in life was to train people. I was born for that.

> There are two good things about reaching rock bottom:
> 1. You can't go any lower.
> 2. The only place you can go is up.

What was the use of my having a tourism company? What was the use of my having worked in the music industry? Well, those experiences made me grow and helped shape who I am today. My work in the music industry taught me to deal with people and do business, while my work in tourism allowed me to take great leaders to Israel and learn to deal with important people. I learned much from these experiences and don't discount the expertise I gained from this work—but I can't deny that my delay in understanding my purpose left me frustrated. That's what happens when purpose is not found. Of course, frustrations also made me gain knowledge that I can now share. Nothing is by chance. However, I could have learned in other ways with less frustration.

When I finally entered into the next phase of life, where I discovered that my mission was training people, it raised a big question: "How will I do that? I have no formal training or knowledge for that." I had the will to do it and a divine confirmation inside me, but I didn't have the means. So, I took the few financial resources I had and decided to invest everything in what I believed to be my purpose in life.

The kingdom of heaven is like a treasure hidden in a field. When a man found it, he hid it again, and then in his joy went and sold all he had and bought that field. (Matthew 13:44)

When you've found your purpose, commit to it fully. Sell everything and invest yourself in it with body and soul, thought and matter, because your purpose will take your life to a new level.

STUCK IN A RUT

In the Disney Pixar movie *Toy Story 4*, a new character joins Woody and his friends: Forky. A young girl named Bonnie built Forky in daycare using recycled materials. When he meets the other toys, Forky is fully convinced he is nothing but a disposable item and, as such, belongs in the garbage.

Woody tries to convince Forky to accept that he is a toy and is destined to have adventures with his owner, Bonnie, and the rest of her toys. However, it is useless. Whenever he sees a garbage can, Forky shouts at the top of his lungs, "I'm trash!" and throws himself into the filth. It is up to Woody, that hero who never gives up on his friends, to rescue him.

One day, Forky is held hostage by an evil toy and comes to understand Woody's words and gestures. When he finally understands his purpose and starts to fight for it, Forky is transformed!

People are like this: until they discover or accept their purpose, they are stuck in trial and error. Don't give up on them. Someday, each word you speak will start to make sense to them, and they will fulfill their purpose in life.

PHASE THREE: DISCOVERY OF PURPOSE

In phase three, everything changes!

There are people who are over fifty but are still in phase two, trial and error. What distinguishes people in phase two from those who successfully complete their life's trail is the discovery of their purpose. When you discover your purpose, you launch a process of making fewer mistakes, listening better, acquiring more wisdom, and focusing only on what you were born to do.

My purpose is to train people. My identity is clear. I already know who I am and what I've got to do. When I first understood this, my life became a lot easier.

Daily we grapple with decisions like,

+ Should I accept or deny this proposal?

+ Who should I hang out with, and who should I stay away from?

+ What's the next step?

These choices and others are made easier for me because I know God's purpose for my life.

As I related in chapter 1 of my book *12 Dias Para Atualizar Sua Vida* [*12 Days to Update Your Life*],[21] there are many ways to approach discovering your purpose. I suggest that you read my book. It will help you as you are searching for your purpose.

An essential idea I address in that chapter is the "Permanent Central Idea (PCI)" that rules your life. All your projects, titles, and dreams revolve around a central idea that is born with you and that will not cease to exist when you die. The permanent central idea of Martin Luther King Jr., for instance, related to social and racial equality. This was born with him and continued echoing even after his death.

---

21. Tiago Brunet, *12 Dias Para Atualizar Sua Vida* (São Paulo: Vida, 2017).

Identify your abilities and what makes you angry, analyze what you say and what people want to hear, and recognize your processes in life, and you will be on your way to unraveling your purpose.

Now I will give you an exercise I use when I help celebrities who, despite their success, feel empty because they don't know their purpose. Fill in these four blanks:

What I Want to Do

_____

What the World Needs	**Purpose**	**What People Want from Me**
_____		_____

My Audience

_____

This exercise has set me on the right track for some time now. Here's what my completed chart looks like:

What I Want to Do

I want to be known as a writer.

What the World Needs	**Purpose**	**What People Want from Me**
The world needs instruction and knowledge.		People see me as a pastor/mentor.

My Audience

My audience is roughly 70 percent Christians (Catholics and Evangelicals) and 30 percent nonreligious people seeking personal development through biblically based instruction.

My purpose was the sum of my prophetic destiny (what God had planned for me) and my natural abilities (gifts and talents). The result of that determined the audience who would stop and listen to me.

So, by applying this tool to myself, I found that I should decrease the energy and financial investment I was applying on being a writer, since my results came from what people expected of me: lectures and sermons. (Notice that I didn't stop producing written content. It took me almost an entire year to write this book, for example. However, I realigned my priorities.) The world needed what I had to offer, and I needed to align all this with the kind of audience that would listen to me.

After completing this exercise, I decided to publicly bolster my image as a spiritual mentor who trains people to achieve their best life. I reorganized my time and investments, prioritizing production and advertising of online videos and relegating books to the background (although writing is still vital to my personal fulfillment and purpose).

Upon doing that, I began to live my destiny intensely!

Take a moment to complete the above exercise. Then, continue reading to discover what comes next.

PHASE FOUR: IMPROVEMENT AND TRAINING

When you discover your life purpose, that doesn't mean you're ready to act on it. In fact, most people don't know what to do to begin fulfilling their newfound purpose. That's why phase four, which we now turn to, is so important.

Let's recap the points we've seen so far on our life's trail:

+ Phase one: Our life's trail starts with learning and role models, when we learn many things and are unconsciously molded by the people in our lives.

+ Phase two: Afterward, we reach the phase of trial and error, when we experience many things but also make many mistakes.

+ Phase three: Then we reach the phase in which we discover our purpose in life. Until this point, we were trying to live somebody else's life; now, we start to live out our own purpose.

Now, with our purpose identified, we reach phase four of our life path: improvement and training.

In my lectures on entrepreneurship and spirituality, I ask class participants this question: "If you were a millionaire and had to hire a bodyguard for your son, would you bring in a SWAT member or an ordinary soldier?"

Most of them reply, "SWAT, of course!"

Then I continue, "And what is the difference between them?"

They all shout, "Training!"

Phase four is all about training. But just as SWAT team training is no picnic, phase four requires real effort and intentionality. In this phase, we will have to pay the price of being polished and remodeled. It's not easy, but this is the path you must walk down to prosper and live a relevant life.

Dear reader, trust me, this phase is vital in the process of becoming a people specialist, as it helps you to understand yourself and those around you. After all, people interpret us according to what we convey.

The level of your training determines the range of your influence.

Invest in learning, role models, and personal growth. You must make your training a priority! Work toward training yourself more than anything else. Your level of training will lead your audience to choose and trust you and will make you stand confident in difficult times. The level of your training determines the range of your influence.

Understand that the investment you're making in phase four is not only financial. You should invest time with people who are new role models to you. You should also invest in knowledge—and, remember, there is much high-quality knowledge you can find for free!

For instance, when I discovered my purpose, I started to walk with people who were already doing what I wanted to do so that I could learn from them. I also started to read five to ten books per month, many of them related to emotional intelligence, coaching, and leadership. In addition, I started to invest in courses, even though, at the time, I had just left behind my emotional and financial breakdown and had few resources to my name.

One particularly valuable step I took was to go out to lunch with people who knew more than I did just so I could learn from them. Remember, it is possible to find role models even as an adult. If you replicate the behaviors of successful people, you will have a better chance of reaching success.

We must also make improvements to our behavior. I, for instance, could not just behave like I wanted to be a coach of people. I had to dress differently, speak differently, talk differently. So, I had to improve not only my knowledge but also my conduct in general.

I should warn you that if you are committed to training yourself, reading books, and striving to develop your intelligence and mental capacity but are married to someone who settles for anything, who doesn't dream, and who is pessimistic, you might find conflict in your two-in-one relationship. You may assume that your spouse doesn't love you, that they aren't a good fit, that they don't care for you properly, and so on. You're living in the phase of training and improvement, but maybe your spouse has not yet found their purpose in life. Don't judge your spouse, but *help* them!

> On your life's trail, value those who make your walk easier.

PHASE FIVE: COMMUNICATION ALIGNMENT

What's the use of finding your purpose in life and training for it if you can't explain it to people? Communication alignment, the next phase, ensures that you are communicating who you are clearly and consistently across all communication platforms: the way you dress, the words you speak, the content you post, and the associations you generate (see chapter 1). Our communication defines us. Attitudes, relationships, clothing, vocabulary, tone of voice—it all contributes to others' perception of us.

As we set out to align our communication, we must keep in mind that our social media—what we post, who we share it with—defines for others who we are. Therefore, we must take particular care over what we share.

What if I were to ask you, "What do you think when you hear the name Tiago Brunet?" You might reply, "Well, he is a wise guy, he helps people, he preaches well; he is an entrepreneur, a family man, an inspiration." (I'm not trying to sound arrogant; these are the kinds of things people say about me daily on social media.)

You see me as a family man. But what would you think of me if I posted a photo of myself in a sports car with my shirt unbuttoned? You see me as an entrepreneur. But what would you think of me if I shared I was having financial problems? You see me as a wise man. But what would you think of me if I kept picking fights with haters online? If I did these things, how long would it take for you to change your mind about me?

Everything you do conveys something. Be careful with that!

Everything you do conveys something. Be careful with that! Our life purpose can be our guide when we're deciding what to post online. Suppose, for instance, that you read an interesting article and are wondering whether to share it with your followers. Before you do, ask yourself: Is the information in this article aligned with my life purpose? If it isn't, and you share it anyway, you may end up confusing your followers, and they may stop following you. Remember, everything you publish on social media defines who you are and determines your audience.

I make these kinds of decisions every day. When I do so, I find it helpful to think first about my followers. For instance, before posting a picture of myself dining with some celebrities at an expensive restaurant, I say to myself, "Will posting this picture add anything positive to the lives of my followers? Will they learn something from it, or do I just want to show them that I'm having a good time?"

ABOVE SUSPICION

Let me share a well-known story. The Bona Dea (or "Good Goddess") party was held at the home of Julius Caesar house on May 1 in 62 BC. During this event, open only to women, participants danced, drank, and took advantage of a temporary reprieve from social expectations of purity and chastity. The celebration was organized by Julius Caesar's second wife, Pompeia, who is recorded as being a young and very beautiful woman.

A certain rich young man, Publius Clodius Pulcher, fell in love with Pompeia and disguised himself as a lyre player in order to attend the party and be near his beloved. Julius Caesar's mother, Aurelia, discovered the disguised intruder before he was able to seduce Pompeia. Nevertheless, all of Rome learned of the scandal.

Caesar promptly decreed his divorce from Pompeia. When he was called to testify against Publius Clodius, however, he said he didn't have anything against him. That caused confusion among the senators. "Why, then, did he divorce his wife?" they asked.

Julius Caesar's answer has since become famous: "Julius Caesar's wife must be above suspicion." It wasn't enough for Julius Caesar's wife to be honest. She also needed to look honest.

It wasn't enough for Julius Caesar's wife to be honest. She also needed to look honest.

I've come to understand that as I fulfill my purpose in life, people will have a certain image of me, and that image will, in turn, define my audience. Thus, I align my communication so that I will neither frustrate nor shock my admirers. For instance, if Jeanine asks me to pick up something from the store, I usually take a moment to get dressed and tidy up my appearance. When she says, "Gosh, you're just going around the corner," I explain to her that people may recognize me and come up to me, so, out of respect for them, I try to look tidy.

On one occasion, we were dining at a private event with the most influential people in the city. I was seated with famous and important individuals. When a photographer came by, I requested that we remove the bottle of wine from the table before he took the picture. I personally don't think it's a sin to drink wine, but I didn't want to risk shocking any of my followers who think differently about it.

Millions of people recognize me as a pastor. I need to align my communication with that role. Do you understand? Yes, we live for others, not just for ourselves. If I cause others to sin because of my attitude, who will be judged?

> "There is no sky without storms, nor roads without accidents. Don't be afraid of life; be afraid of not living it intensely."
> —Augusto Cury

What about you? Have you noticed anything in your lifestyle or communication that needs to be brought into alignment?

PHASE SIX: RESULTS

Only after we have gone through all the previous phases can we arrive at the last one: the much-desired phase of results. In my case, the signs of growth that indicated I had arrived in this final phase included:

+ An increase in the number of invitations I received to lecture.

+ An increase in the number of followers I had on social media.

+ Financial prosperity.

+ An increase in good things that started to come toward me.

Now, I remembered that when I was in the previous phases of my life, I had also seen results and even started to make money; I had long been living in a good place. How, then, could I know the results I was starting to see were a result of phase three and not phase two, trial and error? Well, it's simple. Those results came after I had discovered my purpose. All my previous results, although good, were just temporary. They were transitory. They evaporated like mist on the road in the heat of the sun.

What distinguishes your life in phase two from all the following phases is the discovery of purpose.

Why do I know that the results I'm seeing today are definitive? Why am I certain I will bear fruit for the rest of my life? Because I found my purpose. What distinguishes your life in phase two from all the following phases is the discovery of purpose. The results I saw previously, when I was living as a businessman, were doubtful; they were just part of an attempt. Those I'm seeing now are part of my life purpose.

Let me issue you a warning. It may seem like everything is easy and smooth on this part of the trail, but it won't always be this way. Distractions, temptations, emotional conflict, physical and mental exhaustion, envy, haters, and critics will arise in this phase. It's not easy, really. Just when you start thinking that, finally, after all you've been through, you've reached the time to enjoy life, you find yourself in the phase of exposure, attracting all kinds of complications.

You have no idea of the number of successful leaders who come up to me on a regular basis and say, "I want to give up everything!" When you feel this way, remember your purpose and keep doing what you're doing. Living purposefully was never meant to be easy—but it is fulfilling and true to who you are and who you were meant to be.

WHEN CONFLICT ARISES

Major problems can arise between people who find themselves in two different phases. For instance, we may see conflict when someone who is in the discovery of purpose phase is married to someone who is in the results stage. When someone is trying to focus on and fully understand what they were born to do, it is easy for them to compare themselves to someone who is already reaping the results of their purpose, and to grow frustrated. Emotional maturity, patience, and wisdom also become disconnected in each phase, giving rise to further potential conflicts.

The conflicts we see are not the result of one person pushing aside the other. Rather, they're because one person is in a different stage from their spouse and doesn't properly understand their spouse's struggles at that moment. Gaining a proper understanding of the trail of life and its accompanying phases helps us to empathize with our spouse and avoid stirring up conflict.

We don't just see conflicts in marriage. We can see conflicts arise between friends, coworkers, and relatives walking in different phases. I'm friends with people who differ vastly from me and from each other because they are at different stages of their life's trail. Because I know what phase I'm in, I don't stir things up when we're together. For instance, I'm still close with many of the friends I made in childhood. Each of those friends is living his own life and walking his own path. Some have formed a family, others haven't; some have good jobs, others don't even know what work is. When we're all together, I laugh and bring up the jokes we used to tell; we reminisce about past mischief and the messes we made. I simply try to enjoy these times together. But I rarely speak about my professional life when we're together because I know each of us is living in our own phase. Why should I provoke envy, jealousy, or comparison?

Avoid stirring up unnecessary conflict. When it comes to people in different phases from us, we should apply a similar principle to the one we applied to the three spheres of friendship: let's tailor the information we share according to the other person's current phase. Let's practice maturity and learn once and for all to compartmentalize the information we share.

SPIRITUALITY

It is impossible to proceed through each phase of life's trail without being spiritually connected to Something—or Someone—bigger. I say this not because of my own personal faith, but because it is statistically true.

We are limited, weak, and helpless; we are only human. Jesus Christ is our guide down the path of life. Consider what He says in John 14:6: *"I am the way and the truth and the life. No one comes to the Father except through me."*

Jesus is the way, and if we walk His way, we will reach our final destination: eternity with the Father. That's what I believe and the truth I live for: to preach and announce the good news of salvation.

> Our destiny is eternity. This earth is only a stop on the journey to get there.

Our destiny is eternity. This earth is only a stop on the journey to get there. However, in the Christian faith, the path has as much value as the destination.

It was on the way to Damascus that Paul, previously called Saul, had a vision that changed his path, resulting in his becoming one of the greatest Christian apostles. (See Acts 9.)

It was on the way from Jerusalem to Jericho, according to the parable, that the man known as the "Good Samaritan" stopped to help another man who had been assaulted and left for dead. (See Luke 10:25–37.)

It was on the way to recover his family, who had been kidnapped following an attack on their hometown of Ziklag, that David stopped to help an Egyptian slave, who in turn became a sort of GPS for David, helping him quickly find his enemies, defeat them, and recover his family. (See 1 Samuel 30.)

Spirituality—that is, connection with God—is not just intrapersonal but also interpersonal. The more we help people along the way, the closer we get to God.

> ## We have transformational experiences on life's trail, and it is on life's trail that we also help people.

Think of Jesus's last journey prior to His crucifixion—the path now known as the Via Dolorosa. His body was bloodied, caked with sweat and dirt. He carried the cross on which He would be killed. People around Him shouted and jeered. Guards attacked Him with their words and their fists. It was a path riddled with pain and hardship. Yet when He was nailed to the cross, Jesus stopped thinking of His agony; instead, He sought to help those who were torturing Him, praying, *"Father, forgive them, for they do not know what they are doing"* (Luke 23:34).

This is the level of maturity we need to reach—a level where, as we're trudging down our life's trail, we seek to help others overcome their own obstacles. We have transformational experiences on life's trail, and it is on life's trail that we also help people.

Q & A

Q: Tiago, I participated in the course "Life Trail" in São Paulo, and although I'm known by people throughout the country because of my art, I don't know if that is my purpose in life. After all, I don't feel happy and complete. I have millions of people around me, but I always feel alone. What should I do?

A: Your situation is very common. Succeeding in something that is not our destiny is a risk we all take. We all cling to something that should only be a phase in our lives, not our reason for living. Certainly your art is part of your purpose, but only as a contribution. For instance, a singer's voice is a tool, but his purpose is to transform people's lives through his lyrics and melody. Transformation is a purpose. Music is a tool. I hope this has been helpful to you.

CONCLUSION

Identify which of the six phases presented in this chapter you are currently in, and start to project your future. Then, make a list identifying three people with whom you are close—your spouse, a close friend, a beloved relative—and identify which phase of life you think they are in. This will help you to know yourself and those around you better.

And remember: what divides the "before" and the "after" of your walk here on earth is the discovery of the purpose in life God has given you.

> God usually entrusts big projects
> to small people.

7

LIVING MIRRORS

"All the world's a stage, and all the men and women merely players."
—William Shakespeare

"The world is a stage, but the play is badly cast."
—Oscar Wilde

I'm convinced that we have the power to enhance the good or bad feelings people carry within them. With a simple smile, we are able to improve someone's day. With an impolite comment, we are able to compromise an environment, spoil an atmosphere, and cause hurt feelings.

Each positive attitude we display, each courtesy we offer, is a dose of kindness for someone else. Each complaint, each harsh word, each honk of our car's horn when the light has just turned green, is a dose of bitterness for someone else.

You can stir up feelings that are within people. Be careful what fuel you place on other people's fires.

The song "Epitáfio" ("Epitaph"), made famous by the Brazilian band Titãs, includes these poignant lines:[22]

Each one knows the joy
And the pain he brings in his heart

The people we pass on the street carry pain and joy that only they are aware of. When we bump into another person—someone we don't know, or an acquaintance, perhaps an unavoidable one, or even a strategic friend—we see only their glazed eyes and somber expression. If only there were a kind of portable X-ray device that helped us decipher what was going on within other people! It would even be helpful if we could screen our own feelings, for sometimes we're not able to decipher even ourselves. In my opinion, this is the main reason why we hurt and get hurt.

SCRUTINIZING OURSELVES

Before we continue this journey of becoming a people specialist, let me ask you some important questions: How far are you willing to go to improve as a person? How much are you willing to invest in your happiness so that you will be able to make others happy? How much do you really want to be a people specialist?

Hopefully you are willing to make some changes to your life, because I'm going to share with you an important truth: *People never believe they are part of the problem*—but they usually are! There's something reassuring in the fact that, ever since the world began, people have thought that the problem lies in someone else. I've never been alone in this journey of disillusionment, and neither have you!

Take a look at what the greatest people specialist of all time said:

Do not judge, or you too will be judged. For in the same way you judge others, you will be judged, and with the measure you use, it will be

22. Titãs, "Epitáfio," by Sérgio de Britto Álvares Affonso and Eric Silver, *A Melhor Banda de Todos os Tempos da Última Semana*, Ariola Records, 2011.

measured to you. Why do you look at the speck of sawdust in your broth-
er's eye and pay no attention to the plank in your own eye? How can you
say to your brother, "Let me take the speck out of your eye," when all the
time there is a plank in your own eye? You hypocrite, first take the plank
out of your own eye, and then you will see clearly to remove the speck from
your brother's eye. (Matthew 7:1–5)

Even Jesus, whose gospel I preach and spread, emphasizes that the problem is sometimes you.

Do you want to accuse someone? Look in the mirror.

Do you want to judge someone? Look in the mirror.

Do you want to point your finger at someone? Look in the mirror.

If you want to improve someone, improve yourself.

Rarely do we scrutinize our own behavior as much as we scrutinize that
of others. That's probably because we're unaware of how we act throughout
the day. We can't see our own face or posture during a conversation, nor do we
receive a video compilation of our behavior every evening to review and analyze.

It's easier to complain about having to coexist with difficult people
than to recognize that sometimes we are the source of our own difficulties.
Perhaps you are a little selfish; this is causing you to miss opportunities to
get along well with other people. Perhaps you tend to put money before
friendship; this is causing your friends to feel used. Perhaps you miss family
reunions because you need to work; this is causing your family to deem you
a workaholic.

Yes, sometimes you are the source of your own difficulties. Unfortunately,
the world doesn't work the way you or I want it to. It doesn't spin around the
way you think it does. Anyone who believes he has the truth or insists he is
always right is doomed to fail.

Do you understand what I'm saying? If not, reread this paragraph, please!

If you want to improve someone, improve yourself.

THE HOUSE OF A THOUSAND MIRRORS

A well-known folk tale tells how, long ago, in a small village far away, there was a place known as the House of a Thousand Mirrors.

A happy little dog heard of this place and decided to visit it. When he got there, he frolicked up the stairs to the front door. Then he looked through the door, his little ears pricked and his tail swinging as fast as it could. To his astonishment, he found himself face-to-face with one thousand happy little dogs, all with their ears pricked and their tails swinging as fast as his. He smiled a huge smile and received one thousand grins in return. When he returned home, he thought, "What a wonderful place! I'll visit there again."

In this same village there lived another little dog, who was not nearly as happy as the first one. He too decided to visit the house. He slowly climbed the steps and, disgruntled, looked through the door. He saw one thousand hostile dogs staring back at him. He growled and showed his teeth in response; to his terror, he saw one thousand angry little dogs growling and showing their teeth back at him. As he left, he thought, "What a horrible place. I'll never go back there."

Every face in the world is a mirror. What reflection do you see on the faces of the people you meet?

As I've been saying throughout this book, to become a people specialist, you need to get to know yourself. How? Start your journey toward self-knowledge by completing the following three tasks.

TASK 1:

Before you go to sleep at night, review your day and write down the reflections you raised at first glance from people today...

In traffic: _____

At work: _____

On the street: _____

TASK 2:

When you wake up in the morning, think of a good memory, a favorite song, or a motivational quote. Talk about the memory out loud; sing the song; repeat the quote to yourself. Then, in the evening, reflect on how this morning practice affected your day.

_____

_____

_____

_____

TASK 3:

Conduct a social experiment. Offer a sincere smile to someone you don't know—someone next to you in traffic, seated by you at a restaurant, or in line with you at the store. Take note of the person's reaction.

_____

_____

_____

_____

These tasks seem very simple, don't they? They _are_ simple—but they're effective. Recognizing your emotions and how they affect your day and the day of people around you is vital to becoming a people specialist!

If we want our society to improve, we need to treat people well; the positive changes we make will be reflected in our community.

It's time to change! It's time to change yourself! Judge less! Speak less! Get angry less! Hurt others less!

By making subtle changes to yourself, altering the way you treat others and conduct yourself, you can begin to change the world for the better.

CHARISMA

I hold an annual leadership workshop in Israel. What an overwhelming experience it is to be in the land where the King of Kings was born, lived, and delivered His eternal teachings. Every inch of that land is pure history. Every corner is worthy of a book. Studying leadership in the land where the greatest leader in history shared His teachings is truly remarkable and transforming.

The attendees of this workshop have fun and exchange valuable knowledge during this training time. Many businesspeople, political figures, athletes, and artists have been part of this workshop. We update each other on our lives, create strategic contacts, and have great experiences. The time is truly a gift.

At one of these events, the CEO of a multinational corporation called me over to talk to him as the group was boating across the fantastic Sea of Galilee. He told me, "Tiago, I listen to you because your content is very good and I'm interested in growing. But if I didn't already know of you and were deciding whether to approach you, based on your charm and charisma, I probably wouldn't. In fact, I need to force myself to listen to you because, when I see your rude expression, my heart closes up. Fortunately, when I listen to your words, I understand what is best for me. If you gave a few more smiles throughout the day and greeted more people from the group, perhaps things would improve and everyone would listen to and admire you more."

What? Hello! You mean that years of studying—earning a master's degree and a doctorate—experience, and accumulating knowledge can all be *rejected* because I don't go through life smiling?

Yes. The answer is yes!

I humbly learned my lesson! Based on this experience, I can assure you that your entire professional résumé can be undermined by one thing: lack of charisma.

People are emotional, and if you don't win over their emotions first, your message will never reach their hearts. Human beings want, even unconsciously, to live alongside joyful people—people who are always lively, smiling, and motivated. No one wants to hang out with disappointed people. Nobody wants to hang out with people who seem hopeless.

Forbes magazine, one of the most influential business and economic publications in the world, is so convinced that charisma is essential to leadership that it published an article identifying fifteen ways people can develop charisma.[23]

23. See "15 passos para aumentar seu charisma," *Institute of Business Education*, March 26, 2018, https://www.ibe.edu.br/15-passos-para-aumentar-seu-carisma/.

You can be excellent at what you do and exhibit great character and still be unsuccessful. If excellence and great character were all it took to succeed, malicious and incompetent people never would—but they do. Why? These kinds of people are able to succeed and take advantage of others not because they finished college or are sincere, but because they know how to manipulate people's emotions. They smile, inspire confidence, touch people's hearts, are thoughtful, and master topics that will attract their "victims."

Sympathy makes life easier. Charisma attracts people.

Sympathy makes life easier, and charisma attracts people. Fortunately, malicious and incompetent people don't hold a monopoly on charisma. Men and women who excel in their fields and are people of character can become experts in winning over people too. Let's talk about a few simple things you can do to develop charisma.

A FRIENDLY DEMEANOR

Be friendly. This is not just a tip to get along with people; it is an immutable principle for developing healthy relationships.

I tend to come across as an unfriendly, standoffish person. I recognize it. I don't smile all the time or hug everyone in the room. There is something in me that makes me withdraw when I'm in a room with a lot of people I don't know. I'm dealing with this and have improved over time. I'm also aware that I would be more successful by now if I smiled more. People throughout the world have boycotted my events, thinking I'm lofty or standoffish because I don't hug anyone when I walk into a press conference.

I have tasked the team that travels with me to help me with my demeanor.

Interestingly, I've found that when I don't get at least six hours of sleep or don't eat well throughout the day, my mood changes drastically, and impatience surfaces. If I don't take good care of my physical and emotional needs, I'm more likely to appear stressed and tired when I'm speaking with others. Keeping a smile on my face is challenging considering my routine, though. I spend many nights in airports, and some days I don't eat well because I have too many appointments. But trying to develop a friendly outlook and a positive demeanor is worth it because, when people have a negative experience with someone well-known, they're quick to tell others about it. The better known you become, the more people expect from you. Don't let them down!

> ## The better known you become, the more people expect from you. Don't let them down!

The better known you become, the more people expect from you. Don't let them down!

Being friendly and accessible to outsiders is vital to achieving success in business and in life; being nice and accessible to insiders (i.e., your family members, your spouse, your friends) is vital to being happy.

In my research for this book, I learned that people react emotionally to our facial expressions. There are times when you enter a room and someone you don't even know is already thinking, "I don't like this guy!"

Yes, in general, your facial expression will reveal the state of your heart. At times, this means it works against you. The opposite is also true, as Scripture teaches:

A happy heart makes the face cheerful.   (Proverbs 15:13)

What is in your heart—your emotional state—also determines what your facial expression will be.

So which should we fix: our face or our hearts?

It's tricky, isn't it? Well, cheer up. You're not alone! I'm in this process of self-improvement too. Writing this book has been helpful. What about you? Are you seeing improvement?

CHASING CONGENIALITY

The comedy film *Miss Congeniality* stars Sandra Bullock as Gracie Hart, a coarse and unrefined FBI agent who is tasked with competing in a beauty pageant to prevent a terrorist attack and discover who is threatening the contestants. She hires a beauty pageant coach (played by Michael Caine) to teach her how to dress, walk, and behave like a contestant.

People are like this: they judge us constantly by the way we dress, walk, and behave—or even laugh! A people specialist must learn how to deal with this judgment and adapt accordingly.

You are a mirror, and people will judge what you reflect! Take care with your reflection.

BODY LANGUAGE

A study by the University of California showed that just 7 percent of our communication is based on the words we speak. Our tone of voice makes up 38 percent. The remaining 55 percent comes from body language—the physical expression of our thoughts and feelings.[24]

We've discussed how important—and sometimes challenging—it is to control our tongues. Well, it is *much* easier to control what we say than to control our body language. And controlling our body language is even more important when we consider that people will instinctively copy our body language and be emotionally affected by it, for better or for worse.

Since this way of communication represents over half of our message and impacts those around us, it is important that we learn to identify the signs our bodies are giving. Here are a few:

+ When someone looks upward and to the right, they are creating a mental image.[25]

+ When someone looks upward and to the left, they are recalling an image from memory.[26]

+ When someone looks upward, they are either attempting to remember something or feeling disdain toward what is being said.[27]

---

24. Albert Mehrabian, *Silent Messages: Implicit Communication of Emotions and Attitudes* (Belmont, CA: Wadsworth, 1981).
25. "How to Interpret Body Language: The Importance of the Gaze," Reorganiza, May 2, 2018, https://reorganiza.pt/como-interpretar-linguagem-corporal-olha/.
26. "How to Interpret Body Language: The Importance of the Gaze."
27. "O Que 9 Olhares Significam Interprete O Que A Pessoa Esta Dizendo Pelo Olhar," Vix, https://www.vix.com/pt/bdm/comportamento/o-que-9-olhares-significam-interprete-o-que-a-pessoa-esta-dizendo-pelo-olhar.

+ When someone raises their eyebrows, they are expressing concern, surprise, or fear.[28]

+ When someone laughs with their eyes closed, they are laughing sincerely.[29]

+ When someone taps their foot or shakes their leg, it can indicate that they are upset (although some people do this without being aware of it).[30]

+ When someone purses their lips, they are communicating stress.[31]

This is only a sample of the wide range of information you convey and others receive without either of you saying a word. It's vital that we be aware of our body language!

THE POWER OF A SMILE

One day I had coffee with the king of networking among Brazilians who live or vacation in the United States. I asked him if he had a secret for winning over so many strategic people and becoming their friend. He answered right away, "Smile!"

Have you noticed that one of the requirements for becoming a Hollywood star or a famous actor is having a beautiful smile? Have you noticed how an effective salesman—or one who is committed to reaching his sales quota—will help you with a big smile on his face?

A sincere smile is capable of winning people over. Whoever gets one thing by crying can get ten things by smiling.

Think about what happens when people see a baby. A baby simply arrives at a party, and soon a little crowd gathers around him. Everybody plays with the baby, and when he offers them a toothless smile, they all say, "Oh, how

28. "Linguagem corporal: O que seu corpo pode dizer sobre você," HiperCultura, https://www.hipercultura.com/ linguagem-corporal.

29. "A linguagem corporal dos olhos que você nâo vê," Naoverbal.com, https://www.naoverbal.com.br/a-linguagem-corporal-dos-olhos-que-voce-nao-ve/.

30. Thiago Rodrigues da Rocha, "O que nos contam as expressões corporais?" Cosmo & Caos, August 13, 2012, http://rochaniil.blogspot.com/2012/08/o-que-nos-contam-as-expressoes-corporais.html.

31. "Linguagem corporal: o que seu corpo pode dizer sobre você," HiperCultura, https://www.hipercultura.com/ linguagem-corporal.

cute!" On the other hand, if the baby gets annoyed and cries, everybody rushes away from him. "He must be tired. Let's give him some rest," they say. "Is he hungry? Take your time nursing him."

Smiling works miracles from the cradle onward.

> Whoever gets one thing by crying can get ten things by smiling.

WISDOM FROM THE GREATEST EXPERT

Jesus is the greatest people specialist to have ever existed.

The carpenter from Nazareth didn't study psychology or take a course on coaching; He didn't study theology or management. Yet no one has ever been so interested in helping people as He was. No one has ever known how to deal with people better than He did. Jesus could cut into a human being's soul with mere glances and words.

He was called "Master" by many. This wasn't simply because He taught and shared His knowledge; He earned the title "Master" because He was able to transform the life of whoever crossed His path. No one has ever stayed the same after being with Jesus for even five minutes. But what strikes me the most is that He was able to change the dynamic of any setting. Look at this example of the story of a woman caught in adultery:

The teachers of the law and the Pharisees brought in a woman caught in adultery. They made her stand before the group and said to Jesus, "Teacher, this woman was caught in the act of adultery. In the Law Moses commanded us to stone such women. Now what do you say?" They were using this question as a trap, in order to have a basis for accusing him. But Jesus bent down and started to write on the ground with his finger. When they kept on questioning him, he straightened up and said to them, "Let any one of you who is without sin be the first to throw a stone at her." Again he stooped down and wrote on the ground. At this, those who heard began to go away one at a time, the older ones first, until only Jesus was left, with the woman still standing there. Jesus straightened up and asked her, "Woman, where are they? Has no one condemned you?" "No one, sir," she said. "Then neither do I condemn you," Jesus declared. "Go now and leave your life of sin." (John 8:3–11)

He was the perfect mirror. Jesus's peace amid conflict was contagious! His displays of faith encouraged many. His face reflected His heart; His voice convinced crowds of their destiny; His smile attracted multitudes—men, women, and children alike. But, much more important than that, Jesus had profound compassion for people. And this is the greatest legacy of Christ: love for the neighbor. *"Love your neighbor as yourself"* (Matthew 22:39), He taught.

That's difficult, I know. Dealing with people is quite complicated. I think we all understand that by now! Every day, we leave home to run errands and make ourselves totally vulnerable to emotional terrorist attacks. But Jesus equips us to follow His teaching by offering us examples of how to deal with our neighbors.

ACKNOWLEDGING IGNORANCE

This week I went to drop off my kids at school, and the mother of another student pulled up beside my car and started shouting at me and accusing me of stealing her parking spot. "I had my [expletive] turn signal on! Are you out of your mind?" she screamed, seemingly intent on humiliating me in front of my kids.

I just smiled, admitted I hadn't noticed she was waiting for the spot (which was true), and apologized. My apology wasn't enough for her. She kept yelling. From her behavior, I realized that her problem wasn't me or the parking spot but herself. That realization, however, didn't make me feel any better.

What are we to do with the anger, shame, and embarrassment we feel when we're publicly offended and humiliated? Well, to conduct ourselves appropriately in situations like this, we need to reflect Jesus's example. He taught us the way to have eternal life, but He also taught us how to live well during our time on earth.

In the last chapter we talked about the humiliation and pain Jesus suffered on the way to and during His crucifixion. Even when He was enduring the worst pain of His physical life, nailed to the cross and being mocked by His tormentors, Jesus taught us the ideal way of dealing with people: praying, *"Father, forgive them, for they do not know what they are doing"* (Luke 23:34).

Recognizing that people are emotionally ignorant shields us spiritually.

BIBLICAL WISDOM

I repeat: I know that dealing with people is difficult, but I also know that it's possible.

One of the excerpts from God's Word that inspires me the most in my journey to become a people specialist is in the book of Luke. This short passage has taught me so many principles about how to relate with people:

Then a man named Jairus, a synagogue leader, came and fell at Jesus' feet, pleading with him to come to his house because his only daughter, a girl of about twelve, was dying. As Jesus was on his way, the crowds almost crushed him. And a woman was there who had been subject to bleeding for twelve years, but no one could heal her. She came up behind him and touched the edge of his cloak, and immediately her bleeding stopped. "Who touched me?" Jesus asked. When they all denied it, Peter said, "Master, the people are crowding and pressing against you." But Jesus said, "Someone touched me; I know that power has gone out from me." Then the woman, seeing that she could not go unnoticed, came trembling and fell at his feet. In the presence of all the people, she told why she had touched him and how she had been instantly healed. Then he said to her, "Daughter, your faith has healed you. Go in peace." While Jesus was still speaking, someone came from the house of Jairus, the synagogue leader. "Your daughter is dead," he said. "Don't bother the teacher anymore." Hearing this, Jesus said to Jairus, "Don't be afraid; just believe, and she will be healed." When he arrived at the house of Jairus, he did not let anyone go in with him except Peter, John and James, and the child's father and mother. Meanwhile, all the people were wailing and mourning for her. "Stop wailing," Jesus said. "She is not dead but asleep." They laughed at him, knowing that she was dead. But he took her by the hand and said, "My child, get up!" Her spirit returned, and at once she stood up. Then Jesus told them to give her something to eat. Her parents were astonished, but he ordered them not to tell anyone what had happened.

(Luke 8:41–56)

Here are a few of the insights I take away from this passage:

+ It is important to hear people's needs with a compassionate ear.

+ The people around me in any given moment must be my priority; all the rest will work out at the right time.

+ It's good to bring peace to those who want to approach me but fear the way I and those around me may react.

+ If it is within my power to help someone, I consider it a blessing to hear their story.

+ I won't let anyone lose hope.

+ If God has told me something will happen, it will happen.

+ I may ask people to keep something confidential, but that doesn't mean they won't broadcast the conversation.

I challenge you to search the Bible yourself for more wisdom from the greatest people specialist of all time. Read the Bible daily and learn even more from the example of Jesus and other biblical heroes.

MORTAL ENEMIES OF YOUR RELATIONSHIPS

You probably know someone in your family, from school, or in your workplace who always swims against the tide. You probably know someone who, every single day without fail, has a sad story to tell. You probably know someone who, no matter how much effort you've made, no matter how closely you followed the instructions, will cast you a disapproving look and say, "Is this the best you can do?" And, of course, we can't forget that person who always interrupts whoever is talking to them in order to share about their similar, but more fantastic, experience.

Now consider this: Are you that person?

Is it hard for you to listen to people? Is it difficult for you to praise people? Is it hard for you to recognize when you've done something wrong? These behaviors are what I term the "Mortal Enemies of Relationships":

Mortal Enemies of Relationships	
Emotional Deafness	Refusing to hear anyone
Sentimental Selfishness	Refusing to praise anyone
Spiritual Pride	Refusing to recognize your mistakes

I'm no longer talking about charisma and friendliness; now, I'm offering you some blunt advice about empathy and self-knowledge. In order to develop good relationships and become a people specialist, you must admit when you have a weakness, and you must act intentionally to improve yourself. If you don't, you'll find yourself combating an enemy of your own making. Remember, we are mirrors. Who we are and how we behave shapes the world around us. Consider how each of these mortal enemies ends up shaping your experience:

+ If you don't listen to anybody, you'll end up surrounded by sycophants (and this is assuming you have something to offer; if you don't, you will be left alone).

+ If you find it difficult to offer praise, you'll end up surrounded by people struggling emotionally.

+ If you don't recognize your mistakes, you'll end up surrounded by people making worse mistakes than yours.

Look around you and you'll see that what I'm describing is true! This is usually the way it works. We see this play out in our interactions with unavoidable ones and also in the two-in-one relationship. Good luck with your marriage if you never praise your spouse and constantly refuse to admit when you're wrong. Is it even possible to live at peace with your family members if you refuse to listen to anyone?

Developing self-awareness is a vital starting point, but you can't stop there. Follow these simple tips to vanquish the mortal enemies threatening your relationships:

+ **Vanquishing Emotional Deafness:** When you're having a conversation, put down your phone. Look the other person in the eye and nod from time to time to show you're paying attention to what they are saying.

- **Vanquishing Sentimental Selfishness:** Look for something to sincerely praise, even if it is simply someone's good intentions.

- **Vanquishing Spiritual Pride:** Don't be ashamed to admit your mistakes. That's the way to improve.

EMOTIONAL INFLUENCERS

I have all kinds of friends within my three spheres of friendship (see chapter 1). I have good-natured friends, I have funny friends, and I have friends who are always grumbling and complaining.

I have a friend for every situation. When I'm feeling down and in need of cheering up, I call my funny friend. Just grabbing lunch or coffee with him makes everything better. In several instances, as I've traveled to lectures worldwide, I've covered this friend's travel expenses simply so I'd have someone to talk and laugh with for hours. Life is much lighter this way. We need these people!

When I'm feeling fine and dandy (thank God, I usually am), I call my grumbler friend. These are the times to help improve someone else's day. For instance, I invited my grumbler friend to spend the day with me at a large event that Destiny Institute carried out in São Paulo; he was able to visit backstage, have lunch with me and my team, and so on. This is a high-adrenaline kind of event—the perfect atmosphere for me to show him how worthwhile it is to live a life of joy and that having friends and people around us boosts our level of joy. I wanted to show him that complaining and frowning affects everything and everyone negatively.

> ## We are mirrors with the ability to choose what we will reflect.
> ### —Portuguese proverb

Now, you must be wondering, "Tiago, what does this have to do with me?" To which I reply, "Everything!"

We've already talked about the mortal enemies of relationships, so you know to avoid them. Now, it's time to put into practice your sympathy, compassion, empathy, and self-knowledge, and to transform yourself so that you will improve the lives of the people around you. Once you have made an effort to improve yourself, you will reflect good things to the world, and the world will give equally good things to you.

Do you remember the three tasks I assigned you in the beginning of this chapter? Have you already put them into practice? Have you done them for just a day, or have you decided to incorporate them into your routine? How has it worked for you? If you haven't done them yet, it's about time, right?

Stand up and be a mirror that reflects what is best.

Q & A

Q: I'm taking a course with my husband. We're pastors of a church in Santa Catarina, and our goal is to help people to remain in the faith and understand it better. We've been taking care of this church for five years, and, during this time, many people have hurt me with their words and deeds. They say horrible things about me and falsely accuse me, both to my face and behind my back. Recently, someone accused me of dishonoring my husband by standing up during the message. I'm always friendly, ready to help, and kind, so I don't understand why I'm having these problems. I don't know how to deal with this conflict. When they make false accusations, I get extremely nervous and want to defend myself. It's to the point where, every time someone asks to talk with us, I grow distressed. I wish I could emotionally shield myself. I've been wondering if some of my attitudes provoke this kind of reaction from people. I've realized that all they say about me in fact reflects and reveals who they are. They criticize in me the things they do. As pastors, we're supposed to listen to them— but how can I help these people without feeling so much hurt?

A: Dear pastor, nobody should lead without being sure they have developed emotional intelligence. Why? Because when a leader hurts, she usually affects many people and does great damage. When the leader is hurt (because she is not yet emotionally shielded), she gets discouraged and may cause further damage to those under her leadership.

My advice to you, as I know you are a Christian, is a biblical principle: *"Above all else, guard your heart, for everything you do flows from it"* (Proverbs 4:23). The Bible mentions the word "heart" over nine hundred times as the headquarters of our emotions. It tells us to shield and protect ourselves, to guard our emotions, for everything we do flows from them.

People will continue to hurt you, and you have to be prepared for that.

Let me give you another biblical tip: *"If any of you lacks wisdom, you should ask God, who gives generously to all without finding fault, and it will be given to you"* (James 1:5).

CONCLUSION

In the ideal world, we wouldn't need to think about mirrors in life. All people would be empathetic and full of compassion; they would smile, serve each other, and love their neighbors as themselves. However, in the real world, the majority of people are selfish and proud and don't care about the needs of those around them.

We can't relegate to others the task of improving ourselves. We need to do the hard work of improving ourselves so that we can improve the lives of others and have our own lives improved in return. We must take initiative and choose daily to present on our faces a mirror that will reflect our best to others.

Our time has come. Live differently! Make a difference!

> **Believe me:**
> **the fact that you are still smiling**
> **confounds some people.**

8

THE THREE PILLARS

"Don't grumble because roses have thorns:
rejoice because thorns have roses."
—Author Unknown

We started this book talking about how good it would be if we lived in the ideal world. This world has already existed and was known as the garden of Eden. Picture it with me for a minute. The garden of Eden was the perfect place. The food was perfect. The weather was perfect. People's relationships with God were perfect. Everything was perfect!

And then human beings screwed it all up.

Now picture this real world we live in. It is far from perfect! One of the greatest difficulties we face in this imperfect real world is dealing with other people. Thankfully, we have the Word of God, which has a lot to say about relationships.

Many of us are familiar with Jesus's teachings: we should love one another; we should forgive seventy times seven times (that is, every time); we should seek peace in all situations; we should go the extra mile; we should offer the other cheek to our enemy; and so on. However, it is worth discussing these teachings again because they are simple in theory but difficult in practice. Indeed, dealing with people is a daily challenge for anyone, but especially for those who call Jesus their Savior and long for a promised eternity in heaven with Him.

A few questions come to mind:

+ How are we to love one another?

+ How are we to forgive every time?

+ How are we to seek peace in all situations?

To answer these questions, we must turn to three basic pillars. These pillars are essential for any difficult situation you have with any person in your life, whether it is someone in your three spheres of friendship, your partner in your two-in-one marriage, an unavoidable one (a relative, coworker, neighbor, etc.), or an avoidable one (someone who is not a part of your life on a daily basis, like the server at a restaurant or the lady behind the counter at the airport). Let's learn more about these three basic pillars.

PRAYER

When I was a child, my father would always tell me, "Tiago, prayer is the key to victory." It sounds like a cliché, but it worked for me. I never want to be the losing party, so I've always followed my father's advice and prayed a lot! To this day, my father exhorts me every day to live a life of prayer.

You've probably guessed by now that the first pillar that sustains people and helps solve any situation is prayer.

What is prayer? Put simply, to pray is to consult the One who already knows the future, and that's God. *Wow*! If you could consult someone who knows the outcome of any choice you make and can guide you to the best decision, why wouldn't you? Through prayer, we can seek wisdom from our omniscient Lord. Before we act or adopt any strategy, we should pray to ask God for wisdom, clarity, direction, and signs.

At this point, you might be making excuses, thinking things like, "Well, I don't have a religion," or "Praying is for fanatics," or "I don't like to pray." Bear this in mind: praying doesn't make you part of a religious system. Praying doesn't turn you into a fanatic! Praying doesn't concern what you like or dislike. Praying is a *need* of every human being.

Human beings are body, soul, and spirit. Food fuels the body; emotional intelligence nourishes the soul; prayer is the food of the spirit.

The human body can't survive without water or food. Indeed, according to a report from Healthline, "With no food and no water, the maximum time the body can survive is thought to be about one week."[32] So while you may not like eating lunch every day, and you may not be a fan of vegetables, you don't prevent yourself from nourishing your body because you know you can't live without nourishment. Why would you treat your spirit any differently?

Praying is indispensable. The soul suffers without prayer. And, consequently, all your life suffers.

Yes, prayer is fuel for your soul. When you are facing difficulty, ask God to open your eyes, your ears, and your mind and to calm your heart. Ask God to help you to see the situation you're experiencing the way He sees it. Do not hesitate to ask for tips on how He would solve this situation if it depended exclusively on Him. *Believe me*, He answers.

Several of the concepts of personal development we've discussed throughout this book would be considered secular. This means that, while they align with Christian teachings and beliefs, they aren't exclusive to the Christian way of thinking. They are based on science, and science exists to provide us with tools that enable us to grow. Science adds to and catalyzes our development as human beings, but I know that, without a divine connection, everything becomes void and meaningless. Our human development only reaches its fullness when it searches for eternity.

Everything is easier for those who have divine strength; life becomes lighter. This doesn't mean people who pray to God are free from problems—if only! It means, however, that they have access to ancient divine wisdom—the ultimate source to turn to in times of pain and to consult for guidance. Indeed, I can assure you that, if supporting one another and getting along with others is difficult *with* God, it is impossible without Him.[33]

---

32. Natalie Silver, "How Long Can You Live Without Food?" Healthline, October 13, 2022, https://www.healthline.com/health/food-nutrition/how-long-can-you-live-without-food.
33. Understand that I'm talking about God, not religion. Many religious people live a very heavy life because they don't actually know God; they simply worship the rules men have created on His behalf.

If you want to be a people specialist, you need to pray. Talking with God (which is what prayer really is) has powerful and immediate effects. Do you need an illustration?

Imagine if I were to say to you, "I have an incredible prize for you. I guarantee it will be worth it. However, in order to receive this prize, you will need to carry all this stuff around." I point to a pile of random items that, all together, weigh around twenty pounds. "Once you've carried them around, everything will make sense in your life and you will be much happier," I assure you.

You would probably feel a little nervous at the challenge, but you would also feel excited about receiving that prize. But then you take a closer look at that pile. There are a lot of items there. Can you even hold them in your arms without dropping them? Even if you figured out a way, over time they'd begin to weigh you down. They'd be heavy. It would be painful to carry around that pile of stuff, wouldn't it?

Now imagine I gather up all those small items and pack them into one big rolling suitcase. The total weight is the same. What has changed is that the burden is now a lot easier to carry.

Such is the life of a person who tries to relate with other people without praying, without the Holy Spirit, without putting into practice biblical principles, compared to those who rely on the power of God in their life. With the power of God—prayer—it's easier to carry the weight of our daily life, the weight of other people's shortcomings, and the weight of the mistakes people make that affect us.

It's not about religion. It's about strategic faith.

EMOTIONAL INTELLIGENCE

The second pillar that supports us and helps us to solve any situation is emotional intelligence.

Having emotional intelligence is not denying yourself negative thoughts and feelings. Neither is it blaming yourself for having undesirable thoughts and feelings. Emotional intelligence is recognizing when you are having negative thoughts and feelings and acting in a controlled, healthy way. Indeed, what science calls "emotional intelligence" the Bible refers to as the "*fruit of the Spirit* [which] *is love, joy, peace, forbearance, kindness, goodness, faithfulness, gentleness and self-control"* (Galatians 5:22–23).

> **What science calls "emotional intelligence" the Bible refers to as the *"fruit of the Spirit* (which) *is love, joy, peace, forbearance, kindness, goodness, faithfulness, gentleness and self-control"* (Galatians 5:22–23).**

Unfortunately, negative thoughts and feelings are unavoidable from time to time. As we've said throughout this book, there is a significant difference between the ideal and the real world. In the real world, we would find it simple to follow these instructions from the apostle Paul: *"Finally, brothers and sisters, whatever is true, whatever is noble, whatever is right, whatever is pure, whatever is lovely, whatever is admirable—if anything is excellent or praiseworthy—think about such things"* (Philippians 4:8). In this real world, however, we will inevitably struggle with non-ideal thoughts and feelings.

In a famous study, Harvard professor Daniel Wegner set out to determine why it is so difficult to vanquish unwanted thoughts and feelings. To test whether suppressing unwanted thoughts is in fact difficult, he asked one set of participants to avoid thinking about white bears for five minutes. During that period, if they thought of a white bear, they were to ring a bell. On average, the participants thought of a white bear more than once per minute.[34] Likewise, if I were to tell you, "Don't feel envious," or "Don't think of despicable things," you would probably find it difficult not to dwell on your envy or think about vile things.

Let me offer another illustration. Have you ever been on a diet? One of those restrictive ones, full of prohibitions? If you have, you might have found yourself *dreaming of* the foods your diet forbade: pizza, cake, lasagna, soda, French fries, ice cream, chocolate—all those delights! It makes me think of these song lyrics: "Is everything I like illegal, immoral, or fattening?"[35]

---

34. For a summary of this study, see Lea Winerman, "Suppressing the 'white bears,'" *American Psychological Association* 42, no. 9 (October 2011): 44, https://www.apa.org/monitor/2011/10/unwanted-thoughts.
35. Roberto Carlos, "Ilegal, Imoral ou Engord," 1976 [translation mine].

We don't have a choice when it comes to experiencing negative thoughts. But it turns out that emotional intelligence is something we can choose to have. We might not be able to control what we think and feel, but we can choose not to be trapped by those thoughts and feelings, like a fish on a hook.

Do you understand what I'm saying? Emotional intelligence works like this: you cannot control what happens to you and what other people do, but *you have the ability to control how you react.*

Let me give you some tips to help you develop emotional intelligence.

1. RECOGNIZE YOUR PATTERNS AND AVOID TRIGGERING SITUATIONS THAT MAY UPSET YOU.

Years ago, I decided to take note of every time I got nervous about something and lost control. I drafted out some simple questions:

+ When?
+ With whom?
+ Why?
+ Where?

Soon, something happened that caused me to lash out. I was going to go out with some friends, so I asked Jeanine to transfer a small amount of money to my personal account, since she's the one who manages our resources. At the time, she was busy with something and told me she'd do it when she had time. I exploded with anger and exclaimed, "It's my money!"

It was such a ridiculous and absurd scene that I immediately recognized my error and asked for forgiveness. But I took note and thought through the *when, with whom, why,* and *where* of the episode. After months, I began to see a pattern behind my explosions. They would happen...

+ **When** I wanted to do something that gave me pleasure, like going out with friends or attending a soccer game.
+ **With** my wife.
+ **Why?** Because my wife controlled our financial resources and was setting a limit on me.

+ **Where?** At home.

Using this exercise, I concluded that my trigger was pulled when a pleasure was barred because of money.

Folks, this was liberating!

You only change what you identify!

I realized this trigger was related to the hardships I'd experienced in life. Because I had many financial restrictions as a teenager and young adult, I struggle to emotionally admit that I might be limited because I lack some resource. I also discovered in myself a great tendency toward cowardice, for I never had the courage to react this way with any person other than Jeanine. I only exploded at home with the more fragile member of my two-in-one relationship: my wife.

I am grateful that I took the time to identify my trigger, repent of it, and correct it. *You only change what you identify!*

What about you? Are you ready to perform an emotional checkup on yourself?

Things usually don't fix themselves. You have to stop what you're doing and go fix the problem. Today's unresolved problem becomes tomorrow's giant.

2. TRY TO RATIONALIZE THE SITUATION BY NAMING YOUR THOUGHTS AND FEELINGS.

Be honest with yourself. Name your feelings. Say them out loud, in front of your mirror: "I'm feeling hatred," or "The name of this feeling is anger." Then ask yourself these questions:

+ "Why am I feeling this?"
+ "In relation to whom am I feeling this?"

+ "Is this a real feeling or am I imagining things?"

+ "What should I do next?"

To become a people specialist, you need the fruit of the Spirit to replace the primitive instincts of your flesh. The apostle Paul lists these *"acts of the flesh"* as including *"sexual immorality, impurity and debauchery; idolatry and witchcraft; hatred, discord, jealousy, fits of rage, selfish ambition, dissensions, factions and envy; drunkenness, orgies, and the like"* (Galatians 5:19–21). Surely no one can become a people specialist if *"acts of the flesh"* are more evident in their life than the fruit of the Spirit (i.e., emotional intelligence).

Acts of the Flesh	Fruit of the Spirit
Sexual immorality	Love
Impurity	Joy
Debauchery	Peace
Idolatry	Forbearance
Witchcraft	Kindness
Hatred	Goodness
Discord	Faithfulness
Jealousy	Gentleness
Fits of rage	Self-control
Selfish ambition	
Dissensions	
Factions	
Envy	
Drunkenness	
Orgies	

The difference between irrational animals and human beings is this: humans were created in God's own image and likeness. You've got the power to *reflect* on things and to *decide* to break a cycle of hatred! After all, if history shows us anything, it is that haters never succeed.

Theoretically, you know how to solve each and every situation you encounter. You just need to try to make that theory a reality. In all situations, just ask yourself: "What would Jesus do if He were in my place? How can I imitate the Master in this situation?"

You must act according to your values. Do you know what your values are? Can you list them? Take a minute to do this right now. List all the nonnegotiables. It's so helpful to write them down and keep them in sight.

My Values:
1.
2.
3.
4.
5.

3. SHIFT THE FOCUS.

This step is important.

Give yourself a specified period of time during which to think through a situation, but don't get lost in it. He who plants a lemon tree cannot hope to harvest an orange, right? Likewise, spend your time only on what you want to reap! This is the famous law of reaping and sowing.

Thinking through difficult situations and deciding to react in the best way should not bridge over to complaining and gossiping. There's no use in taking the best course of action but continuing to whine about a situation. Instead, shift the focus!

When you're in a difficult situation, decide how to react, take action, and then focus on something else in your life, preferably something that brings you pleasure and joy. For example, if you find it difficult to deal with an unavoidable one and have decided you're going to endure them only at family parties, take a moment to get used to the idea, then think of a way to reward yourself. Give yourself a gift, such as an afternoon on the couch or a ride in the park, a moment of doing something you like that brings you pleasure.

SURRENDER IS THE BEST DEFENSE

In the Bible, we find teachings that are both challenging and counter-cultural but also time-tested and trustworthy. One of Jesus's most popular and important teachings is known today as the Sermon on the Mount. Take a moment to read through what Jesus teaches us about how to conduct ourselves when we're offended or in conflict:

> *You have heard that it was said, "Eye for eye, and tooth for tooth." But I tell you, do not resist an evil person. If anyone slaps you on the right cheek, turn to them the other cheek also. And if anyone wants to sue you and take your shirt, hand over your coat as well. If anyone forces you to go one mile, go with them two miles. Give to the one who asks you, and do not turn away from the one who wants to borrow from you. You have heard that it was said, "Love your neighbor and hate your enemy." But I tell you, love your enemies and pray for those who persecute you, that you may be children of your Father in heaven. He causes his sun to rise on the evil and the good, and sends rain on the righteous and the unrighteous. If you love those who love you, what reward will you get? Are not even the tax collectors doing that? And if you greet only your own people, what are you doing more than others? Do not even pagans do that? Be perfect, therefore, as your heavenly Father is perfect.* (Matthew 5:38–48)

Notice that Jesus's most famous sermon is about interacting with people. As we try to live by these instructions from Jesus, we get the impression that we will always lose. After all, getting slapped on one cheek and then having to offer our other cheek certainly seems like a loss. In truth, however, we're choosing to surrender this moment to God, and in so doing, we're actually shielding our destiny and nipping in the bud future damage and setbacks.

> ## Notice that Jesus's most famous sermon is about interacting with people.

Choosing not to argue with those who have slapped us across the face doesn't make us fools; it means we've decided to get rid of the pain right then and there. Fighting back is expanding the pain, which may turn it into something lifelong. When we decide not to enter into disputes, we have a 90 percent chance of resolving the conflict.

When you're in a difficult situation that requires you to navigate with emotional intelligence, remember that prayer is the first pillar. Surrender this moment to God. When you do this, you ensure that you have a pure heart as you determine how to proceed. This will enable you to let go of your negative emotions, so you don't end up being like a fish caught on a hook of anger, resentment, and sorrow.

When you surrender, you make it so that you are no longer a target.

The enemy's greatest strategy for tearing a hole in our hearts is offending us. But if you don't allow the offense to enter your heart, if you don't let the enemy in, you won't end up trapped. The same theory applies regarding your actions: don't offend and don't cultivate offenses.

Remember that your soul is not foreign territory. You have control of your emotions.

DIRECT, NONAGGRESSIVE COMMUNICATION

The most difficult reality to face is that there can be a gap between what we say and how others understand us. Who among us has never misinterpreted something? Let the one who has never said something and immediately regretted the way he said it throw the first stone.

Yes, dear readers, communication is a *very important* tool in the construction of relationships. More than a tool, it is a pillar, because it—along with praying and emotional intelligence—supports relationships.

Often, the problem lies not in what we say but in how we say it.

For instance, you may not consider yourself a gossip—someone who spreads gossip or enjoys hearing it. But perhaps you are someone who leaves hints on social media or talks behind someone's back. There's a time and place for offering criticism, and there's a right way to do it. This isn't it.

Jesus, the prime example of a human being and the greatest people specialist of all time, didn't hold back from criticizing people, but He did show us how to criticize people the right way. For instance, when He called the Pharisees a "brood of vipers," He didn't whisper the insult to His disciples behind the Pharisees' backs. No, He said it right to their faces. (See Matthew 23:33.)

If you want to become a people specialist, you will need to learn how to communicate assertively, as Jesus did. Assertive communication is such a broad and important subject that I could write a whole book about it. However, I decided instead to summarize for you the principles I consider the most important for successful communication. My goal is to not be overly theoretical but to offer tools that allow you to deal with the people around you more effectively on a daily basis.

The basic principles of direct, nonaggressive communication are as follows:

1. **Smile whenever you can.** Unless the subject you're talking about is sad, heavy, or too serious, try to smile and be as friendly as you can.

2. **Look people in the eye as you're talking to them.** The eyes are the windows to the soul, and it is through them that you create a connection with someone.

3. **When you need to speak openly with someone and to align your expectations, try to talk in person.** Seeking a face-to-face conversation is particularly important with close friends, necessary friends, and unavoidable ones. People feel important when you try to speak with them in person. If you can't have the conversation face-to-face, make a phone call (since no one seems to do this anymore). Remember, not everybody has the gift of communicating effectively in writing.

4. **When you are trying to align your expectations, use questions and phrases such as the following:**

    + "We have different points of view. How can we reconcile them?"

    + "Tell me how you're feeling. Then I can tell you how I'm feeling."

    + "Can you shed some light on this problem?"

    + "What do you expect from me? Are you ready to hear what I expect from you?"

    + "How could we handle things from now on so that we can understand each other better?"

5. **When you are in a fight or an argument, be objective: remember, he who speaks a lot tends to repent a lot.** Try to use phrases like the following:

    + "I'd like to discuss this subject in a precise and thoughtful way, without being aggressive. Can we reach an agreement?"

    + "I'd like to discuss this point calmly. Please stop provoking me."

    + "Let's not get off topic."

    + "This comment is offensive. I think we will have to finish our conversation here so that we don't get too heated or lose our heads."

At first glance, these communication tools may seem impossible to put into practice. But if you use them intentionally and often, they'll soon become second nature.

Decision → Communication → RESULTS

Decide how you will guide your feelings, your reactions, and your attitudes.

Communicate your thoughts in a certain and direct manner.

Wait for the results!

Q & A

Q: Tiago, I've been watching all your videos on your YouTube channel. You emphasize the issue of finding purpose (as if it were easy), living up to your destiny (as if we know what it is), and having emotional intelligence or the fruit of the Spirit (as you teach it). But my life is proof that these things are not easy to have or live out. I know I need then, but I can't do what must be done. Is there a solution?

A: Dear friend, thank you for accessing my YouTube channel. We receive thousands of testimonies related to each message we post there. Based on what you've said, I can tell you've watched many of our videos.

I do repeatedly emphasize everything you mentioned. Purpose, destiny, and emotional life are vital to our ability to enjoy our earthly existence until our eternal one begins.

If it were easy to find our purpose, to live out our destiny, and to balance our emotions, we all would be beautiful, happy, and healthy. But I'd like to give you three keys that will help you as you seek to fulfill the three pillars above:

- Intimacy with God: talk with God more than with any other person, trust in Him more than in anyone else, and love Him above all else.

- Discipline: repeat daily everything it takes to find purpose, live out your destiny, and acquire emotional intelligence.

- Persistence: never stop or give up; don't get discouraged by daily struggles that arise as you live out the three pillars.

CONCLUSION

The Bible equips us to tackle even the most difficult conflicts we encounter. In the ideal world, we would never argue with others, find ourselves clashing with those around us, or struggle to keep our emotions under control. But this is the real world, and in the real world we will have hardships. We can't control how other people treat us, but we can control how we react in any given situation. The three pillars we discussed in this chapter—prayer; emotional intelligence; and direct, nonaggressive communication—are essential for effectively navigating difficult situations. Don't wait until you're in a difficult situation to put these pillars into practice. Incorporate them into your life and interactions today. That way, when a conflict arises, you'll already be equipped.

CONCLUSION: A LIFE WELL LIVED

"Let no one ever come to you without leaving better and happier."
—Mother Teresa

It took me a considerable amount of time to become a people specialist. But I can assure you that I am what I am because I learned how to deal with people.

As you've read in the pages of this book, I've made many mistakes in my life. If I'd had the emotional intelligence, wisdom, and willingness to listen to counselors in the past that I have today, I probably wouldn't have made so many errors. Of course, I still make mistakes in my relationships with people, but today I know how to correct them, and I seek reconciliation and forgiveness quickly.

That's why I've presented you with this wisdom. If you learn and put into practice what I've shared in this book, your life will improve. I say this with confidence because I know the following is true: *everything is related to people.* If you know how to deal with people, you will have a much happier and easier life.

Let me offer you two precious pieces of advice that are like the icing on the cake. If they seem familiar, it's because they permeate every part of this book. Here they are:

- **Tip 1:** You will never be a people specialist if you don't understand how you yourself function. Know your limitations, your abilities, your traumas, and your strengths. As I always say, "He who does not rule himself cannot rule anyone else."

- **Tip 2:** Stop blaming others. I've emphasized that criticizing your haters and getting back at your tormenters won't change who they are. The liar won't stop lying just because you send him some truths on Facebook. Remember this: it may be the gossiper's fault that they spread news they shouldn't, but you share the blame when you tell secrets to those who shouldn't have access to your heart.

Throughout this book, I've shared precious information like this on how you can become a people specialist. What's more, I've presented to you several relationship theories that will help you protect yourself against attacks that may negatively affect you. Now that you are paying attention to those around you, protecting yourself, and taking time to reflect on what you want from life, the moment has come for me to point you to the single greatest asset on your journey to becoming a people specialist: the Bible.

The Word of God teaches, orients, and leads us to the truth. Its sixty-six books, divided between the Old Testament and the New Testament, show us how to live on earth and how to deal with other people. The Bible's timeless truths offer wisdom that we know is effective because people have been putting it into practice for thousands of years. Its wisdom is tested and guaranteed!

Let's rely on what has already been tested and approved so that we can be confident during the short time we have to live on this earth. To wrap up the book, we'll examine closely the life of one well-known figure from Scripture to see what we can learn from him about living well and finishing life's trail successfully.

ENDING WELL

I recently received a call informing me that an acquaintance, whom I'll call Elaine, had passed away. She was to be buried at four o'clock the following afternoon in Rio de Janeiro. I was traveling at the time, so I couldn't make it. After the burial, I called a mutual friend and asked, "How was Elaine's funeral?"

"I don't know," he replied. "I didn't go."

"How come? Weren't you close to the family?" I asked.

He said, "Tiago, I didn't go to pay my respects to her, and neither did many of her relatives. Elaine was a difficult woman and had made many enemies. People seem relieved that she's gone. Her children are more concerned about their inheritance than their mom's departure."

We will all die someday. We know this, don't we? But the fact is that we live as if this weren't true. Here's the harsh truth, though: the day of your funeral will reveal who you really were during your life. There are those who are buried destitute, and those whose funerals are broadcast live on national television; there are those who are mourned by no one, and those who are mourned by many.

Dear readers, I really believe no one wants to end like Elaine did: alone and unloved, with nobody wanting to honor her. Everybody wants a happy ending. However, this *grand finale* is something we build daily by the way we live. The end of our days on earth is the result of what we did while we still breathed.

> ## The end of our days on earth is the result of what we did while we still breathed.

Scripture gives is an excellent example of someone who finished his earthly life well. Take a look at this death notice:

> He [David] *died at a good old age, having enjoyed long life, wealth and honor. His son Solomon succeeded him as king.*   (1 Chronicles 29:28)

David, the famous king of Israel, died in his old age, without having suffered any terrible diseases, with money in his pocket; he was honored by many people.

You should also know that one of the greatest concerns on the mind of anyone who has built a legacy has to do with their successor: "Who is going to continue what I've done here?" David didn't have this dilemma. When he passed away, his son Solomon took over the kingdom, following in his father's footsteps.

Notice Solomon's words in Ecclesiastes 7:8: "*The end of a matter is better than its beginning.*" David finished his life better than how he began it. Indeed, as is true of every person, this king who had been a shepherd in his youth faced hard battles and struggles throughout his life, and he didn't always make the best choices. He had serious problems with some unavoidable ones, like his wife Michal. She was the daughter of King Saul, and she fell in love with David, the great warrior, and wanted to marry him. However, we see that their marriage wasn't perfect. In 1 Samuel 19:12 we learn that Michal was in possession of an idol, thus presenting a threat to David's commitment to the Lord, and we learn that, later on, she "*despised* [David] *in her heart*" (1 Chronicles 15:29). (See also 1 Samuel 14, 18–19, 25; 2 Samuel 3, 6.)

David also had to navigate some serious scandals and persecutions by his children. For instance, his son Amnon raped his daughter Tamar; then, outraged by this event, his other son Absalom sought to avenge his sister by killing Amnon. (See 2 Samuel 13.)

Indeed, David was intense in everything he did. He was tremendous warrior, skillful with the sword, and he had a deep fear of the Lord and respect for God's will. He wouldn't dare stand in the way of divine guidance. However, his commitment to the Lord didn't prevent him from breaking ethical rules and making choices that today we would consider inconsistent with the Christian life. David's most infamous sin is recorded in 2 Samuel 11–12. We learn that David lusted after Bathsheba, the wife of one of his soldiers, and got her pregnant. David then created a plot to hide the fact that this pregnancy was the result of betrayal: he ordered her husband to be put on the front lines so that he would die in battle. David then married Bathsheba. David was rebuked by God's prophet after these events, and he repented bitterly.

Yes, King David made many mistakes that brought terrible consequences upon himself and the nation of Israel. But what person besides Jesus Christ has never made a mistake? David was human and had impulses, as every human being has. That's why we're studying him: he was one of us.

But he finished well!

A MAN AFTER GOD'S OWN HEART

After all that we read above, it might be difficult to see how someone like David could be a people specialist, let alone earn the title of "a man after God's own heart" (see Acts 13:22). What qualifies him as a people specialist? Well, let's see:

1. David was a king, but he had genuine friends. Jonathan, Saul's son, was the first among many friends. David knew how to keep spheres of friendship. He had close friends as well as necessary and strategic ones.

2. David was powerful, but he practiced simplicity. He would play the harp and dance with joy. He knew that happiness is found in simple things. In many cases, the more complex your life becomes, the more distant happiness becomes.

3. He had many enemies, but he was never defeated. David knew how to form teams to protect himself. The Bible recounts many instances where he was saved by someone from his team. For instance, one of his "mighty men," Abishai, once saved him from an attacking Philistine. (See 2 Samuel 21:17.)

4. He had moments of rage, but he had a contrite heart. David's humility allowed him to recognize his errors quickly, keeping him under God's grace. We see this when the prophet Nathan rebuked him for his actions concerning Bathsheba and her husband. (See 2 Samuel 11–12.)

5. He was often provoked, but he never entered into wars that were not his. For instance, he had the chance to take over the throne of Israel by killing Saul, but he refused to do so.

6. He knew how to deal with the unavoidable ones, as we see in his interactions with his son Absalom, who betrayed him and tried to usurp his throne. (See 2 Samuel 15–17.)

Yes, that little shepherd boy who became a legendary king was an expert on people. David had three characteristics that made him a people specialist:

+ **He didn't speak too much:** David knew how to use silence.

+ **He was humble:** David protected his heart and emotions with a shield of humility.

+ **He feared God above all else.**

Yes, dear friend, David knew how to deal with people! This, to me, was his greatest asset. This, for me, was his best trait.

We must remember that David endured hardships throughout his entire life. Indeed, as an adolescent, David was rejected by his family and mocked by his brothers. He suffered many affronts from his own flesh and blood. Do you know what David did? He focused on the mission he had to carry out instead of letting himself get bogged down by issues with his unavoidable ones. Did you understand?

IRON SHARPENS IRON

During the process of becoming a people specialist, you will get to know many people. Some of them, God Himself will put in your path. Their presence may not be easy or welcome, but that doesn't mean they weren't sent by God. You see, some people will be a comfort to you; others will become confidants. Some will come into your life to challenge you to grow and take the next step. Others will test your patience. Some will hurt you, but, rather than defeating you, they will serve as a lever for your maturity. One thing is sure: no matter who comes into your life, you will be sharpened by them!

As iron sharpens iron, so one person sharpens another. (Proverbs 27:17)

God placed many people in David's path. The majority of them challenged him. We can see that David was a master at turning the other cheek and focusing on the task at hand. Let's look at some examples.

+ When the prophet Samuel came to David's house in search of the next king of Israel, David's father Jesse seemed to forget about David. (See 1 Samuel 16.) Yet we find no indication that David ever forgot his father.

+ When David brought lunch to his brothers on the front lines in the battle against the giant Goliath, they laughed at him because he wanted to fight. Yet we never see David repay that evil. (See 1 Samuel 17.)

+ When he was running away from his father-in-law, Saul, who sought his life, David hid in a cave. When he had the opportunity to take revenge and kill Saul, he chose not to. Instead, he stayed where he was and trained his army. (See 1 Samuel 24.)

+ When Nabal, a wealthy man, refused to feed David's army, David was enraged and wanted to kill him. However, after Nabal's wife, Abigail, made a humble request of David; David was embarrassed by his anger and changed his mind. He later married Abigail. (See 1 Samuel 25.)

+ When David was king, he took Bathsheba as a lover and had her husband, Uriah, killed. The prophet Nathan rebuked David, and David immediately repented and tried to make amends to ensure others were not hurt by his error. (See 2 Samuel 12.)

+ When David was fleeing his son Absalom after Absalom usurped his throne, David encountered a man named Shimei who screamed curses at him and harshly insult him, accusing him of usurping the throne from Saul. David put this gross affront aside. (See 2 Samuel 16–17.)

There are people whom we simply know; others, God introduces to us.

Yet not every person whom God placed in David's life was a burden. God also placed Jonathan in David's path, and Jonathan proved to be a loyal and true friend. He stood with David in his worst moments. However, not all friends are like this. In Psalm 41:9, whose author was David, we read the following: *"Even my close friend, someone I trusted, one who shared my bread, has turned against me."* In this verse, David speaks about other friends who led him to another level of maturity.

I know enduring betrayal and conflict it not easy, but it is the way people learn. People skills are tools that the great biblical heroes used effectively, and they went on to make history. Learning the strategies of being a people specialist allows you to build an end to your life that is much better than your beginning.

CONCLUSION

…giving joyful thanks to the Father, who has qualified you to share in the inheritance of his holy people in the kingdom of light. For he has rescued us from the dominion of darkness and brought us into the kingdom of the Son he loves, in whom we have redemption, the forgiveness of sins. **The Son is the image of the invisible God**, *the firstborn over all creation. For in him all things were created: things in heaven and on earth, visible and invisible, whether thrones or powers or rulers or authorities;* **all things have been created through him and for him**. *He is before all things, and in him all things hold together.*   (Colossians 1:12–17)

What does the phrase *"the image of the invisible God"* mean?

In chapter 7, we discussed how the world reflects back to us what we present to the world. Likewise, Jesus is the reflection of God; He demonstrates what God looks like. However, I would never say that Jesus is a "free sample" of heaven. The image of heaven He offers us wasn't free. No, He paid the highest price so that we could know that eternity is possible. Its cost was the blood of the Son of God, shed on the cross for our sins.

I conclude this book with tears in my eyes as I recognize that my life and all I'm experiencing today would not be possible if Jesus had not forgiven my sins even before I committed them and if He had not shown me the way of surviving here on earth through His biography, the four Gospels.

As I write this, I'm crossing the Pacific, returning home. As I sit in my seat, observing the flight attendants rushing back and forth, an image came to my mind that made me understand all the "rush" in my life. I spend so much time traveling for work that there are days I don't even know what city I am in. There are periods when I can't hold back my tears because I miss my home and my children. There have been so many times when I've looked at myself in a hotel mirror and I wondered, "Why do you do this, man? Live a normal life. Why are you making all this effort?"

On one such occasion, Jesus answered my question: "You do this because that's what I did for you. After I rescued and forgave you, I entrusted to you the mission of saving souls by preaching the gospel and training and inspiring people through your courses, conferences, and books."

More than ready, I replied, "Here am I, Lord!

Today, my mission is to improve people's lives because of *everything* Jesus did for them. According to Scripture, Christ was in eternity, walking on streets of gold, inhabiting celestial mansions, receiving worship twenty-four hours a day from angels and archangels—but He decided to leave all that behind to come to this earth and buy, with His blood, the only thing there was on earth that heaven did not have: *people*!

All was for you and those around you.

I wrote this book, with its goal of helping you become a people specialist, because I believe God will be pleased to see our efforts to care for those He decided to save.

Learn to care for those Jesus decided to save.

Our journey throughout this book has demonstrated that it is difficult to deal with people and that many of them hurt us. We also know that you and I can also be difficult to deal with, and that we hurt God through our sinful decisions—yet God nevertheless loves us and decided to save us.

I would like to wrap up this book by making it clear that there is no other way: we *must* learn to deal with people! We must be humble, patient, and always willing to forgive, for it's not about our feelings or emotions. The *purpose* is divine and eternal, and it's all about saving people.

Technically, Jesus should have been a religious leader, but He resisted this title when He publicly showed that *a person's life is more valuable than any religious law.* Let's return to the story of the woman caught in adultery and see how He handled it.

The teachers of the law and the Pharisees brought in a woman caught in adultery. They made her stand before the group and said to Jesus, "Teacher, this woman was caught in the act of adultery. In the Law Moses commanded us to stone such women. Now what do you say?" They were using this question as a trap, in order to have a basis for accusing him. But Jesus bent down and started to write on the ground with his finger. When they kept on questioning him, he straightened up and said to them, "Let any one of you who is without sin be the first to throw a stone at her." Again he stooped down and wrote on the ground. At this, those who heard began to go away one at a time, the older ones first, until only Jesus was left, with the woman still standing there. Jesus straightened up and asked her, "Woman, where are they? Has no one condemned you?" "No one, sir," she said. "Then neither do I condemn you," Jesus declared. "Go now and leave your life of sin." (John 8:3–11)

Jesus didn't care about religiosity. He cried for people. He committed His time to teaching people. He died on the cross and rose again for us. He did all this to redeem people.

It's all about people.

Become a people specialist!

Love as Jesus loves!

I wish you peace and prosperity.

ABOUT THE AUTHOR

Tiago Brunet is an educator and public speaker committed to helping people achieve peace and prosperity in their lives. He has ministered in more than forty countries, including Israel, Japan, India, the United Arab Emirates, Egypt, and some countries in Europe and Latin America. He is the CEO of the Destiny Institute in Sao Paulo, Brazil, and a business consultant.

He is a theologian who graduated from Florida Christian University in the United States, where he also obtained his master's degree in coaching. He lives in Orlando, Florida, with his wife, Jeanine, and their children: Julia, José, Joaquim, and Jasmim.